THE WAGON AND THE STAR

THE WAGON AND THE STAR

A STUDY OF AMERICAN COMMUNITY INITIATIVE

MARGARET MEAD

·

MURIEL BROWN

RAND McNALLY & COMPANY

Published by arrangement with Curriculum Resources, Inc., which published the original edition
for distribution by the United States Information
Agency.

Foreword

Ever since the signing of the Declaration of Independence, Americans have invested stars with a special, symbolic meaning. On June 14, 1777, the Continental Congress adopted a design for a new national flag, resolving that "The flag of the United States shall be thirteen stripes, alternate red and white, with a union of thirteen stars of white on a blue field, representing a new constellation," one star and one stripe for each of the thirteen states, once the thirteen original colonies. As the nation grew, a new star was added to the flag each time a new state joined the Union.

Over the years, these stars have come to have more and more meaning for the American people. The pioneers, pushing westward in their creaking Conestoga wagons, not only navigated through the wilderness by following the stars; they also saw in them the bright symbols of their hopes and dreams and aspirations. So in the mid-nineteenth century Ralph Waldo Emerson could write "Hitch your wagon to a star" and know that his meaning would be understood by all Americans.

As generation after generation of Americans have reaffirmed their faith in the ideals of the men and women who founded their country, the American sense of initiative and personal responsibility for helping to realize national ideals has become very strong. Even the children understand what this commitment means and grow up absorbing the essence of it. In their homes they hear their elders discuss family, community, state, national, and international affairs. Children see their mothers and fathers working freely and voluntarily, as individuals and as members of groups, to help meet community needs. The children, themselves, become involved in community activities at an early age.

This ongoing process of nation-building, so often taken for granted in the United States, has no exact parallel elsewhere. Here political and social action begins at the grass roots, as the saying goes, in communities where people with common purposes work together toward specific objectives. As citizens concern themselves locally with larger and larger issues, what they do influences decision-making at the highest levels of government. *The Wagon and the Star* analyzes American community initiative and explains how the process works at the local level.

Acknowledgments

The authors of *The Wagon and the Star* are indebted to many people for assistance in the preparation of this book. The descriptions of community programs and national organizations are based on information received from community leaders directly concerned with the programs and from officers of the organizations. Although, in the end, we did not have room for all of the projects we wanted to include, we are deeply grateful to all of our correspondents for the valuable source materials they entrusted to us, and for the many other ways in which they helped us to find the examples of community initiative we were looking for.

Every case history in our text has been read and, if necessary, corrected by someone thoroughly familiar with the facts. For this important service we especially thank W. R. Blackwell, City Manager, Galveston, Texas; Louis H. Goettleman, President of the Haddonfield, New Jersey, Historical Society, and Mr. and Mrs. Lewis W. Barton, members of this society; Mr. and Mrs. Haskell W. Jacobs, community leaders and members of the

Arlington, Virginia, Committee of 100; Elmore McKee, originator of *The People Act* radio series, now helping to train Peace Corps volunteers; J. Wilson Barker, city official, Weatherford, Texas, and Mrs. E. B. Cartwright, community leader and former mayor of Tin Top, Texas; Mr. and Mrs. George E. Bentley, of the Waterford, Virginia, Foundation; the Reverend Leon H. Sullivan, Chairman of the Board, Opportunities Industrialization Center, Philadelphia, Pennsylvania; Fred Ross, formerly of the Chicago Industrial Areas Foundation, Consultant for Guadalupe, Arizona, and Warren C. Haggstrom, Syracuse, New York, Youth Development Center.

For their interest and cooperation, we also thank the representatives of national organizations who helped us obtain and verify information about their programs: Emma Daylor, Executive Secretary, the White-Williams Foundation; Marion T. Connolly, Coordinator of Public Information, National Association for Retarded Children; T. V. Downing, Secretary and Cofounder, Ruritan National; Eva Grant, Editor, *The PTA Magazine;* Ethel W. Jacobs, then Director of Program Services, and Mary H. Fry, Director of Public Relations, National Travelers Aid Association.

We are particularly grateful to the colleagues who worked with us so faithfully on the book itself: Jory Graham and Adelaide Winston for their careful editing; Margaret and Richard Jenne for typing and proofreading two drafts of the manuscript; Jean Ogden of the University of Virginia for sharing so generously the knowledge she has gained through years of reportorial work in the field of community development; Betty Barton, National Institute of Child Health and Human Development, for stimulating suggestions based on her experiences abroad with the American Friends Service Committee and the United States Department of State; the staff of the Handley Memorial Library of Winchester, Virginia, for invaluable assistance in locating reference materials; Marie E. Eichelberger, Louise Panvini, and other members of the staff of the Institute for Intercultural Studies, New York, for the skill with which they coordinated the work on the manuscript.

The Wagon and the Star is part of the program of the Institute for Intercultural Studies. The research for the book was financed, in part, by a grant from the United States government. The present edition has been slightly revised, as of the spring of 1967.

CONTENTS

I The American Concept of Community

The word *community* has several different meanings. It may be applied to a place, to all or part of a village, town, or city. It may also mean a number of people who share the same ideas, beliefs, or professional interests. But there is a common thread of meaning running through all of the definitions. *Always, community means a group of people who share a common concern and are doing something about it.* This is the special sense in which the word is used throughout *The Wagon and the Star*. The task may be large or small, trivial or a matter of life and death, but the concept of community in America always includes the idea of people doing something together that is of concern to all of them, and doing it of their own free will.

There are countless examples of this kind of activity. A group may decide to form a volunteer fire company in a place where there is no other provision for fire protection; or it may decide to publish a magazine, establish a nursery school, work for civil rights, or tackle any of hundreds of different projects. It is true that some groups may become active in ways that other groups resist. But the essence of the democratic process, as Americans understand it, is freedom to start movements that will bring about change. Purposes may conflict, but when people form the habit of working together voluntarily to achieve their various goals, they prepare themselves to meet any challenge.

Even though it took place more than half a century ago, Americans still remember an event that vividly illustrated the importance of citizen initiative in an emergency. In 1900, a tidal wave driven by a hurricane swept over Galveston, Texas. When the winds and waters subsided, six thousand people lay dead in a monstrous heap of ruined buildings half buried in sand. The elected municipal government was unable to cope with this disaster. Nothing useful was done to meet the situation until a group of businessmen, already working on harbor problems, came forward to take charge.

As soon as the crisis was over, this group organized a committee to find out why the existing government had failed and what better form of city administration could be substituted for the one that had proved so inadequate. This study group reported that the problem was official incompetence and proposed that Galveston be governed by a board of qualified men appointed by the governor of Texas. A new, temporary government was set up on this basis, but the people of Galveston wanted to elect their own city commission. A charter granting this right was approved by the Texas State Legislature in 1901 and immediately put into effect.

Other cities and towns in the United States followed the Galveston experiment with interest; evidently the question of how to improve local self-government was concerning people in many places. During the next fifty years, the Galveston plan was tried, studied, and modified in different parts of the United States. Out of this widespread effort to solve a basic political problem came a vigorous new professional field, public administration.

In 1961, Galveston changed its government again, this time to the council-manager plan, a city administration headed by a professional city manager employed by an elected council or commission. Today, more than 2,090 United States and Canadian cities, towns, villages, and counties, at least half of them with populations under 10,000, are using the council-manager form of government.

As the Galveston experience shows, there is tremendous creative power latent in people, human energy waiting to be channeled directly into community action. This is why Americans consider it so important for communities to foster individual and group initiative. Indeed, the essence of American democracy is the concept of the creative individual in the creative community participating freely in the development of his society.

Although it is distinctively American, this concept of democracy did not originate in America. The principle of representative government, which is an integral part of it, came from England and was established in the Jamestown Colony of Virginia in 1619, as we shall see later.

The concept of self-regulation in community life was brought to the New World by the men and women who founded the Plymouth Colony in 1620. These settlers were the Pilgrims, refugees from religious and political persecution in their homeland, England. They came to America because they believed that here in a newly discovered land they could build a new society, away from the harsh demands of a tyrannical church and an equally tyrannical state. This society, they hoped, would be one in which people could grow freely in mind, body, and spirit toward the fulfillment of their potentialities as human beings.

The story of the Plymouth Colony is well-known today. Records of Pilgrim activities were preserved in England and Holland. Even more revealing are letters exchanged and diaries kept at the time by people on both sides of the Atlantic. The journal of William Bradford, who became the governor of Plymouth in 1621, has special historical value. This document not only gives a vivid picture of life in the settlement during the first thirty years of its existence; it also shows in detail how the Pilgrims put their conception of democracy into practice. The following quotations are typical. First of all, realizing the dangers the Pilgrims faced in moving to America, ". . . it was fully decided by the majority to undertake the enterprise, and to prosecute it by the best means they could." Once there, ". . . as time would admit they met and consulted of law and order, both for civil and military government, as seemed suited to their conditions, adding to them from time to time as urgent need demanded." Subsequently, "The time for the election of the officers for the year having come, the number of people having increased and the business of government accordingly, the Governor desired them to change the officials and renew the election and give the Governor more assistants for his help and advice. . . ." Then, despite some seeming inequities, ". . . [the elders] called the company together and conferred with them, and came to the conclusion that the trade should be managed as before, to help to pay the debts. . . ."[1]

In the covenant signed by the Pilgrims[2] before they finally left the Mayflower in the winter of 1621, one senses the full extent of their dedication to their chosen way of life:

In the name of God, Amen. We whose names are underwritten . . . having undertaken . . . a voyage to plant the first colony in the northern parts of Virginia,[3] do by these presents solemnly and mutually in the presence of God, and

---

[1] R. Harold Paget, *Bradford's History of the Plymouth Settlement, 1608-1650, Rendered into Modern English* (New York: E. P. Dutton. 1920).

[2] It should be remembered that the Puritans, who also settled in Massachusetts, came from England in search of religious freedom, but their colony differed from that of the Pilgrims in one important respect. Their community activities were heavily church-dominated and remained so for many years.

[3] All North America not Spanish or French was then called Virginia, so named in honor of Elizabeth, the Virgin Queen of England.

of one another, covenant and combine ourselves into a civil body politic, for our better ordering and preservation, and the furtherance of the ends aforesaid and by virtue hereof to enact, constitute, and frame, such just and equal laws, ordinances, acts, constitutions, and offices, from time to time, as shall be thought most meet and convenient for the general use of the Colony, unto which we promise all due submission and obedience. . . .

From this concept of self-government came the basic design and the inspiration for the growth and development of a new nation "conceived in liberty and dedicated to the proposition that all men are created equal." The dream of the Pilgrims became the star the people of the United States have chosen to follow, and the prairie schooner, the covered wagon in which later settlers crossed the plains, became the symbol of their determination to do so. The principles underlying the organization of this first American community are basic principles of modern American community life: self-regulation; a reciprocal relationship between the individual citizen and the community, each serving the other; a common concern for the good of all.

In spite of its importance in American history, the Plymouth Colony was by no means the first or only settlement in the New World in the seventeenth century. There were many others, some founded by adventurers, some by political refugees, some by commercial companies that obtained land in America by royal gift or purchase. Still others were established by groups in search of religious freedom, coming from France, England, Scotland, Germany, Holland, Sweden, and Spain. Among these were the Huguenots, Puritans, Quakers, Mennonites, Moravians, Covenanters. Each of these early settlements had its own ideals and problems, its own unique relationships with the government of the country to which its founders belonged. The histories of all these settlements are woven into the histories of the states.

---

4 Paget, *op. cit.*

But it was the colony at Plymouth that provided the picture closest to the present American community ideal: a group of people sharing responsibility for creating and regulating their own group life, without a king, without a state church, without a government based on money, privilege, or force of arms.

As they lived and worked together in their new homeland, the Pilgrims gained a feeling of solidarity that gave them strength to endure incredible hardships. Another name for this feeling is *sense of community*. Now, as in colonial times, this sense of community, of belonging, is a basic requirement for successful participation in community life. It usually comes easily to those who live in or move to places where they choose to be.

But today the route into a given community may be taken quite accidentally. A man may find himself looking for work in a strange town because an aunt died and left him a house there. A family living in overcrowded quarters may welcome the chance to get an apartment in a housing project in a part of town that they have never even seen. Lumbermen recruited in many different seaports may be working together on the same forest land. Migrant laborers from many states may pick fruit in the same orchard in California. An ambitious young business executive may buy a home in a particular suburb because the manager of his company advises him to do so for the sake of his career. A family may be living in a house that was once in the middle of a congenial neighborhood and is now surrounded by slums or luxury apartments. People who have spent a great deal of time and money finding a place to live where they can have privacy and space may learn, one day, that the land around them has been sold and that row upon row of little houses will be built upon it.

For these and many other reasons, people may find themselves living, working, playing, and studying among others with whom they have not chosen to do any of these things, in places where they do not particularly want to be. If towns or villages were to be called communities only when they were made up of like-minded people who chose to live together, very few of them would deserve the name. The usual choice today is "Shall I or shall I not do things with those around me that will strengthen the spirit of community in the place where I am?" A community is born as soon as those who live in the same place or work at the same tasks begin to act together.

This is the old principle of *voluntary* commitment, but now it involves new decisions and responsibilities arising from the complexities of modern living. It is much more than simple good citizenship. People who are virtuous, honest, and kind in their behavior certainly help to make a town a desirable place in which to live, or an organization a good group to belong to. But these virtues are not necessarily manifestations of a sense of community or of community spirit.

In American terms, a good citizen pays his taxes, obeys the laws, votes in elections, and respects the rights of others. He keeps up with the important issues of the day and gives money to good causes, such as the Red Cross. He works hard, improves his property, and sends his children to school. He is usually forgiven for minor transgressions, especially if he has found amusing ways of getting around unpopular regulations. His wife may be a good homemaker, a good mother, a good business or professional woman. Everything this man and his wife do may benefit the town they live in and the organizations they belong to. And yet their neighbors may say, "They have no community spirit," meaning that what they do, they do for personal reasons, not primarily for the good of the community. On the other hand, people who neglect their families, never hold a job long, never save a cent, may work with true community spirit for some cause that is significant to them.

This distinction between ordinary civic virtues—loyalty, thrift, obedience to law, industriousness—and voluntary commitment to a chosen task and to the interests of a chosen group is extremely important to Americans. People in other countries whose lives are more or less prescribed by family customs, religious teachings, or governmental decrees may be puzzled by it. They may spend most of their time sharing the tasks, the burdens, the ambitions of others, and yet never experience the feeling of community as Americans know it, the feeling of being totally free to decide for oneself how one will take part in the ongoing life of one's community or group.

The Pilgrims believed local self-government was essential to their new way of life. Most Americans still feel that each community should preserve its independence to the fullest possible extent. Some elected officials may like to "govern" with little or no interference from citizens, but sooner or later this attitude leads to trouble. People with community spirit have a strong sense of personal responsibility for what happens in their communities, and they have many ways of influencing decisions about public policies.

This concern about local government is partly explained by the way in which America was settled and partly by the way the nation has grown. First there were the little settlements, such as Jamestown, Plymouth, and Massachusetts Bay, each isolated and each conducting its own affairs under various arrangements with colonial powers. Then these little settlements were loosely tied together as units of administration from abroad. As the danger of war with the Indians increased, the colonial provinces sought closer relationships with each other. In 1643, four of them—Massachusetts, New Plymouth, Connecticut, and New Haven—formed a federation, the United Colonies of New England.

The preamble of the Articles of Confederation, which set forth the terms of their agreement, describes the hazards the colonists were then facing, and goes on to say, "We therefore conceive it to be our bounden duty without delay to enter into an immediate consociation among ourselves for mutual help and strength in our future concerns, so that in national and religious affairs, as in other respects, we may be and continue to be one, according to the tenor and the true meaning of the ensuing articles."[5]

In these Articles, it is specifically stated that the United Colonies enter into "a true and perpetual league of friendship and amity for offence and defense, mutual advice and succour, upon all just occasions, both for preserving and propagating the truth of the gospel, and for their mutual safety and welfare." It was made quite clear in this document that each of the four colonies, under the governments of Massachusetts, New Plymouth, Connecticut, and New Haven, "shall have separate jurisdiction among themselves in all cases as a complete body . . . separate jurisdiction and government within their limits."[6]

When the American Revolutionary War was over in 1783, the thirteen colonies, now thirteen states, began the long process of national federation. The first form of alliance was a league, with no provision for a strong central government. The states were not considered as members of a single nation, but as a group of separate, newly independent little nations, united in an uneasy coalition under an agreement again called Articles of Confederation. It was not until 1787 that the Constitution of the United States of America was framed by delegates from twelve of the thirteen states. When this Constitution was ratified in 1789 by the majority of states, its provisions went into effect, and the country had a federal government. To this central government the states gave the power to make war and peace and to impose tariffs on imports and exports. But with few exceptions, the first loyalty of the people was to their own states.

---

[5] Paget, *op. cit.*
[6] Paget, *op. cit.*

This loyalty was a sturdy thing, born of the early struggles for survival, toughened by the fight for independence. Later, as new states were formed and entered the Union, each one brought its own sense of identity, achieved through trials not unlike those endured by the original colonies.

Each of these new states began in more or less the same way, as a territory first claimed by a foreign power. Each had assets of great value, and each had its own special problems. Alaska, for example, the forty-ninth state, has an internal situation that reminds one of Massachusetts in the seventeenth century. Alaska covers a larger area than the countries of Belgium, France, Italy, The Netherlands, and Spain combined, but has fewer inhabitants than the Swedish seaport of Malmö. It has busy frontier towns but a practically undeveloped economy. On the other hand, Hawaii, the fiftieth state, has one of the most mixed populations in the world. Its people are of Asian, European, and African descent. Its earliest known colonizers were Polynesians, whose descendants still speak the language of their forefathers. The issues in Hawaii that unite the people there, and make their struggle different, arise from racial diversity and the island economy.

The Civil War was a hard experience for the whole nation. On one side were the northern states, in which slavery had been outlawed; on the other, the southern states, in which slavery had become highly institutionalized. Border states, such as Maryland and Kentucky, were torn apart as some of their citizens sided with the North and others with the South. Psychologically, the end of this war is not yet in sight. The bitterness of defeat united the states of the Southern Confederacy, and victory brought the northern states into new and closer relationships. But the difference in attitude between people who have lived in states in which slavery was once an integral part of the social system and those who have not continues to plague the United States.

In every American community one finds in the attitudes of the people reflections of the historical events that have shaped its destiny. There is the belief that all decisions affecting a group should be made by its members and that outside interference is tyranny, wherever it comes from. Because of the long colonial struggle with imperial governments and ecclesiastical hierarchies abroad, a small American community now is usually just as quick to resent what seems like an undue exercise of power by any larger political unit (a county, the state, or the federal government) as if it were a threat coming from a foreign country. The larger unit must always be reminded: "The power you have is the power we give you. Be careful how you use it!"

There is, too, the feeling for consensus. The influence of the English Quakers on American attitudes toward the management of controversial issues has been very strong. The Quaker method of waiting for a group to reach a consensus of opinion when something has to be decided is a basically democratic process. There are many times, however, when this approach does not seem practical in so large a nation as the United States. Americans, therefore, even in very small groups, usually vote to determine the will of the majority. But minority positions are fiercely protected. Every identifiable group in the United States was once a minority, so, even when a group does constitute a majority, it is apt to act and feel as if it were still a minority that had very recently attained power.

American community life is characterized by a special kind of group dynamics—a struggle from the moment that two or three people begin to act together; a struggle to get going, to keep going, to change direction if need be, to deal with new problems. A town in which no group is struggling about anything gives the impression of lifelessness. But there is also the possibility that the sense of community may be lost by disagreements in a previously like-minded group. There is the fear that cooperation in a group may break down when people with different customs and standards clash, or when others come in who have different purposes. Such struggles need not necessarily destroy a community. It is shared tasks that matter, and a very small endeavor may be enough to start a group on the road to consensus.

With the sense of struggle and the awareness of the possibility of failure, disruption, and loss, there is also, in most Americans, a sense of responsibility for helping where help is needed, for taking initiative when needs are to be met. Since what a person does *with* and *for* his group is a matter of choice, a great many different things can be going on in a community at the same time. One group may be supporting a home for unmarried mothers. Other groups may be trying to stop the sale of liquor, collect money for cancer research, enlarge a library, straighten a dangerous curve in a road, revise the electoral system of the United States, establish a hospital in a faraway land, or stop the building of a new high school because they think that two new primary schools are needed more. Still other groups may be offering courses in flower arrangement, campaigning to protect wild animals or to lengthen the hunting season, sending help to earthquake victims in Yugoslavia, Chile, or Japan, fighting to change the form of city government, or working for the United Nations. And so it goes. Big causes and little ones jostle each other because there is a general understanding among the American people that when someone thinks he sees something that needs to be done, he should go ahead and try to do it.

There is also the feeling that those best able to handle a problem are the people on the spot, where the problem exists. But there is no inconsistency in the fact that a service club—a group like Kiwanis, Ruritan, the Lions Club, or Rotary International—may be financing a boys' club in some distant country and buying uniforms for the local basketball team at the same time. As a group with a common interest in the development of international leadership, they help the foreign boys' club. As public-spirited citizens who are proud of their own boys and want them to look well when they play, they buy the uniforms for the local team.

So, behind the American sense of community is the belief that work of the community and the world is done by groups of people who act together to reach a common goal. There is no limitation at all on what the goal may be. Nothing is too difficult, too big, or too little for a determined group of people to undertake. The group needs no mandate except its own sense of responsibility.

This is the spirit in which the Pilgrims signed the Mayflower Compact as their storm-beaten ship lay at anchor in Cape Cod harbor. After more than three hundred years, it is still, more clearly than ever, the spirit of American community life. The poet Robert Frost put the essence of this spirit, this sense of community, in a couplet of ten words:

> Let me be the one
> To do what is done.

II

Towns— Settings for Community Development

From the eastern seaboard, the colonists and their descendants spread out over the continent. Sometimes they made their way in groups of several families of like-minded people. Sometimes a man alone or a man and his family would start out to seek a better fortune. Sooner or later, a number of families would decide to stop at or near the same place, and a new settlement would come into existence. Sometimes this settlement would be a stockade, or a village built compactly, so that it could be easily defended. Sometimes it would only be a random cluster of scattered homesteads or farms on the prairie.

Although most of these settlements finally turned into self-governing communities by following a similar series of steps, the settlements themselves were almost unbelievably diverse. This was partly because the circumstances that led to the founding of each were so different. When people built, they had to consider the climate, the contours of the land, the nature of the soil, the presence or absence of pure water, and the building materials at hand. Three of these requirements, for example, determined the choice, in 1744, of the site for Fredericktown, now Winchester, in the Shenandoah Valley of Virginia. According to a local historian:

It was located directly on the old Indian trail, later to become "the great waggon road" which traversed the Shenandoah Valley from north to south, and from which minor trails branched eastward over the Blue Ridge Mountains . . . and westward over the Alleghenies. It was also close to a cluster of bold limestone springs which guaranteed an abundant supply of pure water in a rocky terrain where well-digging was expensive and difficult. It was, in addition, situated in a heavily wooded area, all of the first homes and buildings being constructed of logs which had been cut on their sites.[1]

There were, of course, different kinds of towns in colonial America, just as there are today. In Pennsylvania, the province of William Penn, the great English Quaker leader, the first settlements were often built in the traditional European fashion around a market square. As the southern colonies from Virginia to Louisiana divided their territories into administrative units called counties (parishes in Louisiana), a town in each county was chosen to be the seat of county government. Each of these county seat towns built a courthouse, where the business of the county was transacted. These stately buildings became symbols of democracy, as important in the Old South as the town meetinghouse was in New England, a fact often overlooked because so much has been written about another aspect of southern culture, the aristocratic old plantations, beautiful, indeed, but built and maintained with slave labor.

Into the Far West—Arizona, New Mexico, and California—the early settlers (Spanish priests) brought Spanish architecture. Sand-colored adobe and red tiles replaced the wood, stone, and brick used as building ma-

---

[1] Garland R. Quarles, "Historic Winchester in Virginia," *The Ironworker*, published by the Lynchburg Foundry Company, Lynchburg, Virginia, Vol. XIX, No. 3 (Summer, 1955).

terials on the East Coast and in the Midwest. Towns were built around central plazas dominated by mission churches or cathedrals. When the Easterners came, they were charmed by the sweep of wide arches, the cloisters with their rows of columns, and the palm trees that shaded walkways from the sun. Guadalupe, Arizona (discussed in Chapter V), is such a town. It is surrounded by crumbling earth-brown walls, and the bell tower of a Spanish mission still rises against the bright blue sky.

In the nineteenth century came the "cow towns," now familiar to millions of people all over the world who have seen American westerns. These towns were hastily built and were all more or less alike—stores, hotels, and boarding houses, bars, the sheriff's office and the jail, on two sides of a dusty main street lined with watering troughs and hitching posts for horses. The period of American history in which these towns flourished is surprisingly recent. Most of them began as convenient stopping places for men driving herds of cattle to northern and eastern markets from the great ranches in Kansas, Oklahoma, Wyoming, and Texas. Texas entered the Union in 1845, Kansas in 1861, Wyoming in 1890, and Oklahoma in 1907.

Americans delight in regional differences in towns of the past and present. But it is the idealized memory of the small New England villages where the first descendants of the Pilgrims and the Puritans lived that is still the dream of what a small town should be: elm-shaded streets; a village green or common, with a white wooden church at one end and a hall for town meetings at the other; white houses in gardens with white picket fences; a little school house; an inn or tavern; a jail for disturbers of the peace; a pond with ducks on the water. In winter, snow falls gently over this peaceful scene. The school is ungraded. The teacher is a neighbor's daughter. The doctor is the friend and confidant of every family. Everyone speaks his mind at town meetings. There is a volunteer fire company, and a single village constable to deal with stray dogs and an occasional law-breaker.

This image is a fantasy now, because there are very few places that fit the description anywhere in the United States today. But it is a persistent fantasy, and it seems to become more dear to Americans as the years go by. The legend is expressed in the paintings of many American artists and in restored colonial towns like Williamsburg, Virginia. Year after year, this legend is the theme of American Christmas cards. It is the setting for stories of early American life that are read by children everywhere in the United States, whether they live on the hot plains of central Texas, in the manufacturing towns of modern industrial Massachusetts, among the live oaks of Louisiana, on the slopes of the Rocky Mountains, or in the fertile valleys of California.

The parents of some of the children who read about life in colonial New England may never have learned to read or write. A town meeting may be as foreign to them as a rite from a strange religion. In their worship, they may kneel in an old Spanish mission, or sing in Greek or Syriac, or study the Koran or the sayings of the Buddha. Some of them may be American Indians who still call upon the spirits that were supposed to have brought rain to their ancestors in times of drought.

The children may go to a consolidated school which serves so many villages that no one community feels any special responsibility for it. The teachers may be strangers, coming from far away each morning and returning to their distant homes as soon as classes are over in the afternoon. There may be no local doctor; the only way to get medical help may be to ride in a car or truck to a hospital 50 miles away. In many places there will never be snow, and Christmas Day may be hot instead of cold. But nostalgia for a way of life that seems to have been so friendly and *right* keeps the image of the legendary New England village alive and even preserves some of its customs in the most unlikely places.

The facts of New England life were often quite different. Many New England villages clung to barren hillsides, where stones were the best harvest the steep fields could yield. Gradually, people in these difficult hills gave up trying to keep cattle fed and warm through the long, cold, New England winters and gave up trying to make a living from the resisting soil. They went away, leaving behind them gaunt, deserted houses, and barnyards stacked with broken farm implements. Many of the once busy little towns where New England farmers traded are today almost as deserted as the farms. When the automobile came, it made life possible for some of the families who stayed. They could make a living in nearby mills or factories by driving back and forth to work each day.

Some of the surviving colonial villages have been taken over by such talented people as painters, writers, musicians, actors, and scholars, who appreciate the architecture of a quieter age and want to live where they can enjoy it. In many of these villages now there are summer theaters, where young people try out their acting talents before audiences made up of people on holiday from faraway New York, Philadelphia, or Chicago. Other New England towns have become winter vacation resorts. A few, like Deerfield, Massachusetts, have been preserved as historical monuments.

Most of America's villages, towns, and cities have been shaped primarily by the way the people who live in them make their living. There are towns where tin, copper, silver, gold, or coal are mined. There are towns where people tell time by the whistles at the mills or the mines. There are railroad towns, where freight cars clang across switches all day and all night. There are quiet, rural villages. There are great industrial centers like Pittsburgh, Pennsylvania. There are single-industry towns like Hollywood, California. There are huge transportation centers like Chicago, Illinois.

The extremely rapid growth of the population of the

United States in the past fifty years has been another factor tending to change and diversify American communities. In 1910, there were 91,972,266 people in the United States. By 1960, this number had risen to 179,323,175, including Alaska and Hawaii. In 1910, there were only three cities with populations of 1,000,000 or more; in 1960, there were five. So fast are American urban centers growing that before long there will probably be one long, continuous, metropolitan complex from Boston, Massachusetts, to Norfolk, Virginia, on the East Coast, and from San Diego to San Francisco, California, perhaps even to Portland, Oregon, on the West Coast. Increases in the number of villages, towns, and cities in each census category, between 1910 and 1960, are shown in the table following.

GROWTH OF THE POPULATION OF THE UNITED STATES, 1910–1960, AS REFLECTED IN THE INCREASE IN THE NUMBER OF VILLAGES, TOWNS, AND CITIES OF DIFFERENT SIZES.[2]

LOCAL POPULATIONS	NUMBER OF POPULATION CENTERS	
	1910 Census	1960 Census
1,000,000 or more	3	5
500,000–1,000,000	5	16
250,000–500,000	11	30
100,000–250,000	31	80
50,000–100,000	59	203
25,000–50,000	119	427
10,000–25,000	369	1,146
5,000–10,000	605	1,326
2,500–5,000	1,060	1,789
1,000–2,500	2,717	3,545
Under 1,000	9,113	9,873
Totals	14,092	18,440

In old American cities, there was a good deal of separation between the rich and the poor and between

[2] From the 1960 Report of the Bureau of the Census, U.S. Department of Commerce.

old residents and immigrants. But as long as the horse was the only means of transportation, the employer and his employee, the shopkeeper and his customer, the man who owned a carriage and his groom and coachman, the mill owner and the mill hand, all had to live within a comparatively short distance of each other. Even if one lived in splendor and the other in poverty, they walked the same streets, knew each other by sight and by name. They worked, lived, played, shopped, voted, and went to church—if they went to church—in each other's company.

All this began to change with the advent of power-driven forms of transportation—the streetcar, bus, private automobile, commuter train, and plane. Manufacturers and businessmen found that they could have their factories and offices in one place and their homes in another. They also discovered that certain types of commercial activities could be concentrated in certain specific areas. Parts of cities became more and more differentiated, until today every large American city has highly specialized sections, like the garment-making and the Wall Street financial districts of New York City, or a ring of suburbs where women and children spend their lives, and husbands and fathers are at home only in the evenings and on weekends.

Suburbs are towns that owe their existence to the fact that trains, buses, and privately owned automobiles make it possible for people to live at a distance from the offices and factories where they work. There are new suburbs, old suburbs, and suburbs that have both old and new sections. Many of the new suburbs are big housing developments where small, neat, box-like houses stretch for miles. Sometimes the only difference between one house and another is the color of the front door. These little dwellings remind one of the words of the Chinese philosopher Li Po: "Of all those ten thousand houses by the willowed river, fair sweet lady, which is the little one you call home?"

There can be, and often is, a sense of community even where a suburb has not grown slowly but has been mass-produced almost overnight. The management strives for order; the parents and children strive for normal family living. Sometimes housing project dwellers form citizens' associations to protect their interests; sometimes they act spontaneously to deal with immediate issues. In one community, the owners of a large modern housing development sent workmen in the night to remove all clothes poles from the area; they considered these unsightly. Word of what had been done spread rapidly from house to house. The next morning, mothers appeared with baskets full of freshly washed children's clothes. Methodically, they draped these garments over the shrubbery to dry, until every bush and low tree in the project blossomed with little shirts, overalls, panties, nightgowns, and diapers. The clotheslines came back as quickly as they had disappeared.

Old suburbs have a different look. New kinds of light industry have come to many of them, including scientific research centers supported by government agencies or large commercial concerns. In such communities, there are usually adequate schools, auditoriums where people can meet, churches, libraries, country clubs, hospitals, and organizations that carry on a variety of programs and stimulate interest in national and international issues. Many suburbs are a combination of the old and the new, with perhaps an old village as the center of the new development. The political power may still lie with an old regime; new residents may lack, at first, any form of organization to deal with controversial matters. Sooner or later, however, a sense of community helps factions to resolve their differences. One of the most famous encounters between entrenched politicians and newcomers in the history of American community action took place about twenty years ago in Arlington, Virginia, near Washington, D.C. The story of what happened there is told in Chapter IV.

A number of things have happened to many cities as more and more people have moved out to the quieter, less crowded suburbs. As urban populations have dwindled, so have local sources of financial support. Even more serious may be the loss of local leadership. There are certain men and women on whom the American community system has always depended, men and women whose lives are oriented to the present and future welfare of their children, people who have the time and education to work for this future. These people are natural community leaders. Without their imagination, organizing ability, and initiative, the neighborhoods they have forsaken have less stability and less ability to plan and take charge of their own community activities.

In many instances, these former residents have been replaced by migrants from less privileged parts of the country, who are unused to city life and unskilled in the ways of city living. Many of these new arrivals have moved into once-elegant mansions abandoned by their previous owners. Others move into tenements and public housing projects. Miles of low-cost, high-rise apartments can now be seen in New York City, from the windows of the United Nations building.

Much has already been learned from these new situations about the sense of community and how it develops under different conditions. It has been found, for instance, that a 1,000-family apartment dwelling hardly ever becomes one community. All the residents of a single floor can become a community, but it rarely happens that the people living in different wings or on different floors can achieve this. Thus separated, they do not usually know each other well enough to share common concerns or to have special reasons for wanting to work together. We have not yet learned how to help people who live in tall apartment buildings to relate to each other as families once did when they lived in houses set along a street.

The rehabilitation of the inner city is a problem which preoccupies many groups—citizens, city planners, politicians, and businessmen. Indeed, the problems of metropolitan areas have become so acute and so complex that a new Federal Department of Housing and Urban Affairs was created in 1965 to help states and cities deal with them.

Clearly, any resemblance between the colonial village on the Christmas cards and the villages, towns, and cities of modern America is very slight. People in other countries may well ask: What is the effect of picturing as the ideal American community a kind of town that only existed briefly, in one particular part of the country, and did not survive even there? There is an answer to this question: A principal effect of this emphasis on an image has been to keep the ideal separate from the realities of everyday community life. This is very important because the dynamics of growth are somewhere in the margin of difference between dream and reality. The pioneers followed their star to the west in wagons that were earthbound, under conditions always far less than ideal.

This separation between dream and reality is probably what people mean when they say that Americans are incurable idealists, sentimentalists who are always talking about an ideal *as if it were really attainable.* The traditional New England village has become such an ideal, not because of its delightful appearance but because of what it symbolizes. There has been a long and continuing struggle to separate the essentials of the ideal of community from the New England pattern so that the essentials can be made to work anywhere in any of the states of the United States, in subtropical Hawaii as well as in arctic Alaska, on the wide plains of the Midwest or in the Deep South. "Anywhere" also means "in any setting"—in towns where flattopped, commercial buildings stand in ugly rows on treeless streets; in "poverty pockets"; in prosperous villages; in small towns taken over by military bases; within cities and in the sprawling suburbs which now fill up so much of America's once wide and empty landscape.

Many of the older challenges to the first settlers have been met. It is hard to find a community today that is really isolated. As a farmer feeds his stock, he is more than likely to be listening to news of the world on a transistorized pocket radio. In the evening, he and his family watch the same television programs that are being viewed, at the same time, by millions of other families. Standard forms of foods and drugs are widely distributed. Cars are everywhere. Highway traffic roars, night and day, through villages that used to be as remote as Guadalupe. Modern machinery, helicopters, and rescue trucks now do much for communities that neighbors used to do for each other.

But there are new problems—the need to make individual communities less self-centered; the need to make the suburbs into real communities, where people can know each other and have a sense of belonging; the need to restore and revitalize the centers of old cities. With perhaps a higher priority even than these is the need to equalize opportunities for work and education thoughout the nation, thus making it possible for everyone, including those who never before have had such a chance, to gain the knowledge and the skills necessary for coping with the problems of modern living.

Intensive efforts are now being made to deal with the most pressing of these problems through new and imaginative programs of social, economic, and political action. Although there is increasing emphasis on the role of the federal government in the development of these programs, *every one of them is community-based* and depends for its success on local community initiative. Every village and town in the United States will make its own unique contribution to this national effort; nationwide commitment to American ideals and values will unify them.

III

The People of the United States

Even more diverse than American villages, towns, and cities are the American people. The population stream of the United States has been fed, from the beginning, by different racial streams from all over the world. America, as the late President Kennedy said, is a nation of immigrants.

There were French, English, and Scottish fur traders in northern New England as early as the mid-1500's. Roman Catholic Spaniards founded Saint Augustine, Florida, in 1565. Before 1650, Roman Catholic and Protestant French, as well as Protestant and Roman Catholic English, established colonies along the Atlantic Coast from the present state of Maine to Florida; Hollanders and Swedes made their first settlements on the mid-Atlantic seaboard.

Between 1650 and 1750, Welshmen and Germans came to Pennsylvania, and Covenanters from Scotland, and Scotch-Irish from Ireland, the latter moving into the counties of western Pennsylvania and down the Shenandoah Valley into Virginia, the Carolinas, and Georgia.

Swiss and Germans settled in North Carolina, and the French founded colonies along the Gulf of Mexico. A number of groups seeking religious freedom also came during the seventeenth century. Among them were Quakers from England, Huguenots from France, Mennonites from The Netherlands and Germany, and Moravians, originally from Bohemia. In 1769, Franciscan monks founded the first Spanish mission at San Diego, California.

All of these settlers *chose* to come to America. From the beginning, however, there were large numbers of people in some of the colonies who were not there voluntarily. These were the African Negroes, brought by slave traders for sale to the colonists up and down the coast. A few were sold in the northern colonies at first, but slavery was outlawed in all Quaker communities in 1727, and in all of the northern states, beginning with Vermont in 1777 and ending with New Jersey in 1804. The bulk of the slave trading was with southern planters, who needed the Negroes for the hard, hot work in the cotton and sugarcane fields.

To all of the colonists, the native American Indians were foreigners. How the Indians felt toward white men largely depended on how they were treated. The Quakers, for example, were especially careful to respect the rights of the Indians, and the Indians, in return, helped them learn how to live in the wilderness. Engraved on a stone marker in West Haddonfield, New Jersey, is a tribute paid to the Quakers of West Jersey by an old Indian chief: "Not one drop of our blood have you spilled in battle, not an acre of our land have you taken but with our consent." Relations between the Plymouth colonists and the Indians in Massachusetts were equally cordial until tribal jealousies and treachery on the part of some white men in the settlement, whom the Pilgrims could not control, aroused antagonisms that helped to bring on the long and terrible Indian wars in the second half of the eighteenth century.

The goal of the Spanish priests in California was

to convert the desert Indians to Christianity. They also organized the Indians as laborers, taught them to care for the mission lands, and used them for construction work. The Spaniards brought horses with them to the New World, but many of these animals escaped to the plains and went wild. The Plains Indian culture came into existence with the arrival of these horses, an indirect result of the colonizing from Europe. Indians who had previously lived and hunted in the woodlands moved permanently out onto the plains, where they formed new kinds of Indian communities. Here, for a brief hundred years, they over-hunted the buffalo, made war against each other and against the advancing colonists, and finally went down to defeat. The Plains Indian had his moment of glory, nevertheless. On horseback, in gorgeously feathered war bonnet, armed with a gun as well as with a bow and arrow, he is an enduring and picturesque image. Although most of the world now thinks of him as the typical American Indian, he represents only one of the many Indian cultures, one that developed late in American Indian history.

The English, Scotch, French, Swedes, Africans, Spaniards, and indigenous American Indians were the principal ethnic and religious groups on the continent at the end of the colonial period, but they were not to be the only actors in the drama as American history continued to unfold. The pioneers going west scarcely had time to settle into their new ways of life when immigrants from other European countries began to pour into the United States, coming for different, usually urgent, reasons.

These reasons were chiefly economic during most of the nineteenth century. Scandinavian farmers, discouraged with farming conditions at home, traveled thousands of miles and endured great hardships so they could still be farmers. They brought to the north central part of the United States, particularly to the states of Wisconsin and Minnesota, their own ancestral version of sturdy independence and self-sufficiency. The Irish, driven from their homes by famine, brought the proud traditions of their little island, where half the inhabitants claim to be descended from kings. The Italians came to earn money as laborers, money they could take or send back to relieve the distress in their poverty-stricken villages. The Poles settled in cities, remained clannish, united by their memories of Polish glory. They are often still regarded as foreigners by their neighbors, even though the third generation has been graduated from local high schools. Eastern European Jews, fleeing from persecution, crowded into American cities.

While Europeans were pouring into cities of the East Coast, Chinese and Japanese were entering the country on the West Coast, for similar economic reasons. The Chinese worked on the railroads, lived in their own sections of San Francisco and New York, maintained their own Chinese identity, managed their own affairs, and kept out of contact with American law.

The Japanese reacted differently. They came as immigrant agricultural workers to Hawaii and California, happy to be free from the cultural pressures that had weighed heavily on them at home. They fitted so smoothly into the racially mixed Hawaiian scene that, in spite of the attack on Pearl Harbor, no need was felt there to isolate them when war came between the United States and Japan. This demonstration of peaceful integration is one of the important contributions the new state of Hawaii is still making to the further development of an increasingly complex American culture.

On the West Coast of the United States at the beginning of World War II the situation was far more difficult. Here the Japanese were proud to be living in America. Their children, educated in American schools, thought and felt like Americans. However, these Japanese had confined themselves rather closely to their own communities and were disliked, distrusted, and envied for their agricultural skill by many old Californians, the descendants of people who had themselves traveled a long way to find a land so golden.

The hostility of these older inhabitants reached a climax in 1941, following the attack on Pearl Harbor. Japanese-American citizens were interned in camps, called War Relocation Centers, where they were housed in new, hastily constructed, barracks-like buildings that superficially resembled concentration camps for political prisoners in other parts of the world.

Many people in the United States were violently opposed to this high-handed way of dealing with people in our midst who were from a country against which we had declared war. Through organizations they belonged to, these Americans volunteered to work in the camps to help uprooted Japanese families rebuild their lives. Japanese men and women who were qualified and wanted to enlist in the Armed Forces of the United States were permitted to do so. Arrangements were made by the United States government to return to Japan those individuals and families who wished to go back. Centers were established throughout the nation to find homes and work for those Japanese who could leave the camps.

Japanese college students were sent to institutions of higher learning in nearly every state. One boy entering a midwestern university was elected president of the student body the day after he arrived. The crucial part of this resettlement work was done in the communities into which the Japanese were moved. Local leaders in small towns and cities took upon themselves the task of preparing the way, so that local residents would be ready to welcome the incoming strangers. Within a remarkably short time after the close of World War II, Japanese-Americans were again free citizens, free to move where they would.

With the exception of this wartime episode, most of the people who came from other lands to the United States in the second half of the nineteenth century, looking for freedom from want, found places for themselves in the American economy. One such immigrant group after another suffered as newcomers, sent their children to school, earned enough money to be able to move into better homes, and left their old houses to newcomers less skilled and poorer than they. This is the old and continuing story of the changing American scene.

Ellis Island in New York Harbor, though now closed, was once the gateway to the United States for millions of immigrants. European immigration has slowed to a trickle, partly because many of the needy peoples of Europe can now find political freedom and profitable employment nearer home, partly because of restrictive American legislation in 1921, 1924, and 1952.[1]

In the last 125 years, political crises in one nation after another have brought requests for political asylum in the United States from people of many nationalities. Among the first political refugees to arrive in large numbers were the German liberals who left Germany when their bid for freedom failed in 1848. They brightened the American cities where they settled with traditions of good music, good food, and good fellowship. They built concert halls and opera houses and convinced their neighbors that music was an essential part of community life. The idea of municipally supported music, originally a very German idea, is associated, in the United States, with cities like Cincinnati and Milwaukee, which have large German elements in their populations. Like the New England town meeting and the court house in the small southern town, the civic orchestra is now an established institution in many American communities where there never was a German settlement.

In the 1930's and 1940's there were streams of refugees from Nazi Germany and the smaller countries

---

[1] Many of these restrictions were removed in 1965 by amendments to the McCarran-Walter Act of 1952. The new law is the result of a careful study of all previous legislation affecting immigration to the United States. It provides, among other changes, for the complete elimination of the old quota system by June 30, 1968.

conquered by Adolf Hitler. Most of these newcomers were sophisticated city dwellers who have enriched the intellectual, scientific, and artistic life of the United States by their presence. The organizations set up to help them find homes and suitable employment are now dissolved because their services are no longer needed.

A problem of similar urgency developed in 1956, when the Hungarian revolt failed. The United States received and helped relocate several thousand political refugees who had escaped into Austria. In the 1960's, a large number of Cubans who rebelled against the Castro regime fled to the United States. Special programs to aid them were organized through the joint efforts of public and private agencies.

"The trouble with the United States," an Englishman once said to a visiting American lecturer, "is that you have too many foreigners over there," meaning "too many people who are not from the British Isles." This sentiment is often echoed in America by people who never had even one English ancestor. Sometimes even American Indians, whose forebears came from Asia, pay lip service to the myth that the real Americans came from the British Isles, and refer to England as "the old country."

As immigrants from Europe, Latin America, Asia, and Africa make themselves at home in the United States, they think of themselves as Americans and speak of still newer immigrants as foreigners. In an effort to become assimilated as quickly as possible, members of a new group may try to get rid of traditional costumes and manners that make them seem different. Later, when they feel secure in their new citizenship and can again take pride in their origins, it is hard to reconstruct the old songs and dances that have been forgotten, or to replace the native costumes that were thrown away when the need to look and act like Americans was so strong.

There is always the possibility that new arrivals may overwhelm the communities where they settle and make it difficult, if not impossible, for the older inhabitants to maintain what they consider the American way of life. Experience has shown, however, that American democracy flourishes best in communities where strangers from many places have come to live and have been well received. It is hardest to maintain the democratic process in isolated places where two racially different populations are linked economically but live socially separate lives. White Americans and Negro Americans, or Caucasian Americans and Mexicans, or Mexicans and a remnant of some American Indian tribe may be living close together. When the two groups face each other with a sense of difference undiluted by the presence of any third element and aggravated by differences in wealth or education, it is hardest to form a unified community.

In the struggle to integrate people from so many different countries, a complicating factor has been the contrast in physical appearance between the early English settlers and the other people who are Americans today. The early English settlers were, indeed, the founders of the Republic, the spiritual ancestors of every American citizen, but only a few Americans can now actually claim to be descended from them.

The Pilgrims were physically similar. They were northern Europeans, with characteristic hair and fair skins. But how to group Americans today is a problem that has baffled the Census Bureau for years. The present census categories, based on color, are almost meaningless. People who are listed as "white" are people who claim only European ancestry. The strange category "Not nonwhite" was invented for people who obviously have other than European ancestry but want to make it clear that this "other" is not an African strain; American Indian, perhaps.

There is a continuing struggle to minimize these distinctions and to emphasize that all American citizens are Americans. Sometimes the effort to underscore this fact takes extreme forms, like the advertisement in the New

York subway that shows a bright-eyed little Negro boy eating a piece of rye bread with obvious relish. The message on the poster is, "You don't have to be Jewish to like Levi's rye bread." There is also the widely publicized story of a family who adopted two children, a boy and a girl. The little girl soon showed signs of some African ancestry. "What can we do to make this child happy in our family?" the adoptive parents wondered. After much thought and consideration, they decided to adopt another baby, this time one of Japanese ancestry. This made their family international, a family in which all three children could live comfortably.

The question of how those who are different are to be accepted has been a problem in the United States from the beginning. As one such problem is solved—how to accept Irish Catholics into a Protestant community, for example—a new one is presented: How to accept Asians or Americans of mixed African and European descent into a community where everyone else's ancestors were all European.

Today comfortably situated people sometimes refuse to accept the migrants from poverty-stricken regions who are pouring into the cities looking for work, or at least for food, even when these migrants are clearly of British stock. To these city dwellers, migrants from remote rural areas are foreigners, people who don't yet belong, people who may disturb the tenor of community life, swamp the schools with children who have been ill-taught and ill-fed. In a country where everyone was once an immigrant, the feeling is strong for becoming, as rapidly as possible, someone who belongs, someone who can call later immigrants "strangers." A way of life just attained is hard to maintain, easily threatened.

These massive internal migrations are a growing problem in the United States today. Actually, they began during World War I, when war industries brought workers from rural communities to the places where the factories were located. They remind one, somewhat, of the migrations of the nineteenth century but are, in fact, very different. The immigrants from Europe came with energy and hope, leaving behind their bitterness and poverty and their feelings of oppression and frustration. The pioneers, rolling westward in their wagon trains, had the world before them.

The new internal migrants are, for the most part, people who have been Americans for generations. They are Negro Americans from depressed and segregated areas of the Old South and white families from lonely valleys in the rugged Appalachian Mountains, to which their ancestors retreated two hundred years ago. They are also miners of British descent who have spent their lives in American mining towns, not realizing until the mines closed down that there was any other way of life. They are also a second generation of refugees whose parents and grandparents in the 1930's left small farms ruined by drought and repeated crop failures. And they are Puerto Ricans, American citizens but not yet of America, escaping from their crowded island with its transitional economy.

These are the new immigrants, traveling from city to city in old cars, secondhand trucks, and homemade trailers, looking for work and places to live. Sometimes they settle down temporarily, as hundreds of families from the eastern Appalachian Mountains have recently done in Chicago. Perhaps because they represent pockets of poverty, failure, and despair within the United States, they sometimes receive even less of a welcome than the hordes of illiterate, poor, hungry immigrants who crowded the ships crossing the Atlantic in the nineteenth and twentieth centuries.

The problems created by an influx of these rootless families are problems that very few communities can handle alone. New kinds of economic and educational opportunities must be provided in the places where the people live who need them. Under the Economic Opportunities Act of 1964, the states and the federal government are making a full-scale attack on this kind of poverty in the nation. Initial approaches that already seem promising include centers for the training of unskilled workers of all ages; programs of compensatory education for young children from deprived homes; and the development of appropriate industries in regions where new employment opportunities are needed.

The United States has entered another phase of the long struggle to provide equal opportunity for all of its people.

IV Community Development

Community development in the United States is a
long, persistent struggle to realize ideals in terms of
values that are not only important locally but harmonize
with the traditional goals and values of the nation as a
whole. All community activities in this struggle involve
decisions that are the end result of prolonged exchanges
of feelings and opinions between individuals, voluntary
groups of citizens, and representatives of government.
And the accepted American way of reaching community
decisions when people differ about matters of common
concern is by voting, regardless of whether the vote is
cast by members of a voluntary organization in a small
private meeting, or by citizens going to the polls to cast
their ballots in a national election.

Every American citizen has the right to vote if he
or she is of voting age[1] and meets the residence requirements of the district and county in the state where he
wants to vote. If a voter has moved too recently, he must

---

[1] In 46 of the 50 states and the District of Columbia, the minimum voting age
is 21; in Alaska, 19; in Georgia and Kentucky, 18; and in Hawaii, 20.

wait to vote until he has established his new legal residence or else travel back to his former home. If he is too far away to vote in person, he can vote by mail.

The whole system of American government rests upon the right of each citizen to vote, and to vote secretly, free from the pressure of eyes and voices that may be too close and too insistent. No one is required to vote, and some people never do. The importance of voting is felt most keenly by the young man or woman just come of age, by the woman whose mother fought for women's suffrage, by the immigrant who is not yet a citizen but wants to be, by Negro Americans who until recently were barred from the polls in some states by taxes they could not pay or by a literacy test they could not pass.[2]

The right to vote is a corollary of the two basic principles of American government: self-government and representation. The principle of representative government was first applied in America in Jamestown, Virginia, in 1619, a year before the Pilgrims landed. The Virginia colony then consisted of eleven boroughs and plantations strung out along the James River. In April, 1619, the governor of the colony, Sir George Yeardley, announced that a general assembly would henceforth be held yearly, by permission of His Majesty James I and the Virginia Company of London, financial backers of the colony. At this assembly would be present

> . . . the Governor and Counsell with two Burgesses from each Plantation freely to be elected by the inhabitants thereof; this Assembly to have power to make and ordaine whatsoever lawes and orders should by them be thought good and profittable for our subsistence.

Everyone voted in these elections except women, children, and underage apprentices. Drums at daybreak on July 30, 1619, called the twenty-two elected burgesses to the first meeting of the Virginia General Assembly, held in a little wooden church on Jamestown

---

[2] These discriminatory practices were outlawed by the Civil Rights Act of 1964, the Voting Rights Act of 1965, and the Supreme Court decision of March, 1966.

Island. At the very moment when this assembly was meeting for the first time, the Pilgrims were preparing to come to America, bringing with them their concept of local autonomy, which did not then include the idea of representation. These two political principles—as much local autonomy as possible and fair representation in any larger unit of government—are complementary. One without the other is incomplete.

As complete local autonomy became less feasible, representation became crucial. Each American community, as it has grown, has had to struggle to maintain some kind of balance between local independence and the duties and privileges of membership in the county, the state, the nation, and now the world. The issue of local autonomy is still very much alive as small, outlying towns fight against being included in the great cities of which they are now necessarily a part. It occurs whenever cities fight against the encroachments of the state or demand more financial aid from the state. It arises whenever a state must decide whether to accept or refuse subsidies from the federal government that might interfere with its freedom.

In the history of each little town and village, this struggle to become an efficient, self-governing community is part of the past and part of the present. The sense of identity within these communities comes from their awareness of what they once were and of how they have grown and changed. Where the cities of Asia, for example, look back 2,500 years to the invasions of conquerors, such as Genghis Khan, and preserve the ruins of palaces these conquerors destroyed, only a handful of American towns and cities can look back as far as three centuries; most are scarcely one century old.

Thus, most Americans have a sense of growth and change that is very different from that of people whose cities underwent centuries of invasion, destruction, rebuilding and more invasion, destruction, and rebuilding. Their feeling is also different from that of people, such as herdsmen, or villagers traveling in carts drawn by oxen, who have been swept out of their peaceful, isolated worlds into the Space Age.

Although their accomplishments have to be judged by what has happened within a period of time that must seem very short to people in older countries, Americans, too, like to remember where they have been in order to think about where they are going. This is why American communities are always having anniversary celebrations —centennials, sesquicentennials, memorial services, historical pageants, Fourth of July parades. These celebrations give them opportunities to reinterpret their past, note their achievements, and generate energy for new developments.

Celebrations, town meetings, and elections are all part of the struggle for growth and survival that goes on in every community. The following descriptions of four actual places in the United States—a borough,[3] a village, a town, and a county—show how dramatically communities can change in the course of this struggle.

HADDONFIELD | Three Centuries of Quiet Progress

Across the Delaware River from Philadelphia, Pennsylvania, is the borough of Haddonfield, New Jersey. Its present population is about 13,200. Originally settled by Quakers, it is still thought of as a Quaker town, although many people who are not Quakers live there. It began with Elizabeth Haddon, a young Quakeress who came to New Jersey in the year 1701 at the age of twenty, to claim land belonging to her father. Elizabeth's first home was built on a hilltop pasture called Haddon's field. The village that grew up around the Haddon estates became the Haddonfield of today.

---

[3] In certain states, including New Jersey, an incorporated municipality smaller than a city is called a borough.

When Haddonfield was preparing to celebrate its 250th anniversary, in 1963, committees of the local historical society fanned out in all directions to gather facts for a commemorative history of the borough. The people on these committees found their materials in diaries and letters handed down in families, in old newspapers, in public and private documents. Their book, *This Is Haddonfield,*[4] represents not only a valuable kind of community project, but also has considerable sociological value because of the intimate picture it gives of what happened as Haddonfield grew.

This Is Haddonfield shows how the first settlers met their needs for food, clothing, and shelter; what they built and where; how paths through the forest became roads, then streets, then highways; how community services were organized; how the government was enlarged from a little town meeting to a modern city administration; how voluntary societies and organizations came into existence locally and increased in number; how private and public agencies with similar concerns found ways of working together; how the community grew out of its original isolation into an ever-widening circle of state, national and international relationships.

All of the story cannot be told here, but a quick look at developments in three major areas of community life—business, community services, and government—will be enough to show how local initiative transformed a wilderness settlement into a modern town.

At first, Haddonfield consisted of three buildings: Elizabeth Haddon's house, a gristmill, and a blacksmith's shop. One by one, other families came, especially after a Friends (Quaker) meetinghouse was built nearby on land donated by Elizabeth's father. Their dwellings were spacious homes, surrounded by fruit trees and gardens. Each estate had its own outbuildings—stables, woodshed, smokehouse for curing meats, milk and cheese

---
[4] The Historical Society of Haddonfield. *This is Haddonfield* (Haddonfield, New Jersey. The Society, 1963).

house, distillery, house for making cider and vinegar, and a pigpen. Each family produced most of what it needed, and in addition some of the villagers set up little businesses to supply general needs, such as shoes for people and horses, mills to cut lumber and grind corn. There was no apothecary shop until 1775. The first plaster mill was built in 1778.

By 1834, there were one hundred dwellings in Haddonfield, seven stores, two taverns, two gristmills, two tanneries, and a woolen mill. The transition from the self-contained, self-regulating work life of the original estates to mass production and consumption, to the impersonality of modern department stores, grocery chains, and organized municipal services had begun.

By 1861, there were enough businesses and industries in Haddonfield to require the publication of a business directory. The little craft shops that were such an intimate part of earlier home and village life vanished, one by one, and were almost all gone by 1880. In 1945, the business community had grown to the point where it needed self-regulation, and both a Better Business Bureau and a business association were organized.

For a long time, the Haddonfield community was small enough to give friendly, personal assistance to any member who needed help. As the population increased, it became essential to organize community-wide programs of social service to aid families in distress. These programs, as in most other American towns, are now carried on by both public and private agencies staffed with professional workers. However, nowhere in the United States does the responsibility for meeting all the welfare needs of the community rest on these agencies alone. In Haddonfield, as elsewhere, residents still keep track of human needs and quietly meet many emergencies as private individuals, as members of voluntary service groups, or as volunteers working directly with the public welfare organizations of the borough.

Until Haddonfield was incorporated as a borough

in 1875, such community services as fire protection and snow removal were performed voluntarily. In 1764, a group of Haddonfield men organized the Friendship Fire Company, the second oldest in America today. The company bought its own equipment until it came under the control of the borough commissioners in 1875. Now the borough owns most of the fire-fighting apparatus, provides a paid chief and four paid firemen in addition to the volunteers, and houses the company in a handsome modern building at the former location. In a letter to a local newspaper in 1875, a subscriber wrote: "The people of Haddonfield are under obligation to Messrs. John Gill and Benjamin Willis for their public spirit in sending snow ploughs through the town after each fall of snow and opening the sidewalks. Mr. Gill attends to the upper part of the town and Mr. Willis the other end."

Haddonfield's present form of local government has evolved partly in response to the changing needs of a growing community and partly to changes in the political framework—the complex of township, county, and state governments of which the borough is an integral part. In the beginning, the Friends Meeting was the seat of authority. Here, after the religious service was over, matters of business were brought up. When Haddonfield was big enough to need a more formal arrangement for managing village affairs, its business was transacted in town meetings called for that purpose.

In the eighteenth century, as now, the Quaker way of arriving at decisions in meetings was to prolong discussion until everyone who wanted to speak had been heard. If there was a dissatisfied minority in a village meeting, a decision would usually be postponed. When a consensus was reached (called by Quakers the "sense of the meeting"), responsibility for carrying out agreements was placed in the hands of an individual or committee. The committee is not only a typical Quaker way of doing business; the English practice of working through committees has become customary for all kinds of American organizations, public and private.

Town meetings are still held in Haddonfield, but these assemblies no longer function as governing bodies. During the last 100 years, Haddonfield citizens have tried several different forms of local municipal administration. In 1875, when the village was incorporated as a borough, it was governed by eight commissioners, one of whom was chosen by the others to be president. In 1898, Haddonfield changed to the mayor-council form of government and gave this up in 1913 for the commission form made popular by Galveston, Texas. In 1958, an elected charter commission recommended a return to the mayor-council plan, but the citizens voted to continue with the commission plan and are still using it.[5]

Local, state, and federal governments are closely related in the United States. Issues over such matters as road building, taxes, or government grants for local improvements constantly arise between local, county, state, and federal jurisdictions in all American communities. When a new interstate highway goes through a village, does the community help pay for it? On what basis? When a city street leaves the town and becomes a country road, how is the cost shared for upkeep and repairs? When the federal government allocates money to the states for roads, schools, or social welfare, how do these funds get to the communities? Who administers them, and with how much authority, at the local level? Does federal money mean federal control? Answers to such questions have to be worked out cooperatively, and it takes time and effort to make the basic issues clear.

American communities deal with these and similar matters in different ways. In Haddonfield, thoughtful problem-solving, generation after generation, has re-

---

[5] It is taken for granted in the United States that citizens have a right to accept or reject the recommendations of representative exploratory groups. Reexamination of the findings and conclusions of experts is an essential part of the democratic process.

sulted in steady growth. On the other hand, there are some municipalities that do not seem to have the inner strength necessary for this kind of development. The village described next in this chapter is 150 years old and has not yet achieved a sense of community.

SPRINGDALE | Village in a Trap

Surrounded by fields and wooded hills, Springdale[6] is a country village in upper New York State with a population of about one thousand. It looks a little like the image of the New England colonial village—freshly painted white houses, neat yards, church spires, a beautiful stream, and no moving picture theaters or supermarkets to spoil the illusion. Standing out among the other buildings is a big, modern school.

Springdale was a quiet place until the state put a highway through the middle of it. Now trucks rumble down the main street, but the village has the same empty look it has had for years. Except when the children are rushing home from school or families from nearby farms are doing their Saturday shopping, there are few people about. The motorist who stops occasionally for food or gasoline may have to hunt for someone to serve him, and he probably wonders, as he reenters the stream of traffic, how a place that is actually in today's world can seem to be so far out of it.

The village began in 1793 as a collection of scattered homes in the wilderness, established by soldiers mustered out of colonial armies. These first settlers were soon joined by families of Congregationalists from Connecti-

---

[6] Springdale is a fictitious name given to this village by two sociologists who studied community life there in the mid-1950's. The following description of Springdale is based on the findings of this research. For a full report of the study see Arthur J. Vidich and Joseph Bensman, *Small Town in Mass Society* (Princeton: Princeton University Press, 1958), reprinted, 1960, as an Anchor Book (paperback edition) by Doubleday & Co., Inc., Garden City, New York.

cut, devoutly religious people of English ancestry. A number of small settlements were founded, and several of these were organized into a township called Springdale in 1811. Two settlements in the new township, on opposite banks of a little stream, were combined to form Springdale Village. These two hamlets were rivals and insisted on remaining as separate as possible, even to the point of maintaining separate public services. To this day, Springdale has two shopping centers and two fire companies.

From the beginning, Springdale Village has been a trading and service center for the township and the surrounding countryside. Its history reflects the economic changes that have taken place in the region during the last 150 years. At first, the main industry was lumbering. Gradually the land was cleared, and the people turned to general farming. The farms were small, but for a while they yielded a good living. Soon, however, Springdale farmers found that they could not compete in the open market with the great farms and ranches of the Midwest and Far West. By 1920, most of the farms in the township had been sold to strangers—Polish and Ukrainian immigrants, German farmers who had not been successful in the Midwest, and Springdale merchants who had failed in business.

Springdale, meanwhile, had been developing as a small industrial village. A railroad, completed in 1834, brought regular deliveries of mail and newspapers. The coming of the railroad also meant that industries dependent on outside sources for raw materials and markets could now be started in the village and the township. By 1875, Springdale had a chartered bank, three hotels, a wool factory, two flour mills, two blacksmith shops, two wagon repair shops, a foundry, three local newspapers, and a telegraph office.

But this prosperity did not last. The small businesses and industries that had begun with so much promise failed, one by one, unable to hold their own against such modern developments as mass production and the mail-order houses. And then the gasoline engine, which had all but destroyed the economy of Springdale, provided the basis for its reorganization. Farm tractors, milk trucks, and mechanized milking equipment made dairy farming and fluid milk transportation possible. Along came free rural mail delivery, radios, and private cars to take people far and wide for business and pleasure.

The economic depression of the 1930's brought real disaster to Springdale. Business in the village slowed once more to a standstill. Relief checks, relief work, pension checks, and other forms of relief were for a time the only source of income for many families. And again strangers came to take advantage of opportunities to buy property at cheap prices. Among these newcomers were Finnish farmers who knew how to cope with marginal land. Also settling in the township were vagrants, who built a shack town on the outskirts of the village.

Conditions began to improve locally in the late 1930's with the establishment of federal government subsidies to maintain fair prices for milk. Then came World War II and many regional war industries. Workers poured in from other places. Villagers found out-of-town jobs and commuted to work. Village stores were all occupied again. Churches and other public buildings were repaired and repainted. Even the shack town looked better, brightened by flower gardens during the day and electric lights at night. Springdale was a thriving trading center once more, this time for a transformed agricultural area. A milk-collecting plant was set up in the village. Farm implement dealers and grain merchants are now the leading businessmen.

Without some knowledge of this background, it would be hard to understand Springdale today. The impression of tranquility given by the village is misleading because behind this façade there is intense activity. The authors of *Small Town in Mass Society* paint a fascinating picture of this inner world. The most striking things about it are its detachment and the self-satisfaction of the people who live in the glow of the image of themselves they have created.

Out of touch with the main currents of thought and action in the state, the nation, and the world, Springdalers nevertheless have the feeling that they can choose the best our civilization has to offer and ignore the rest. They have convinced themselves that theirs is the finest community in the state, a model of what a rural community should be—a friendly place where everyone accepts, likes, and respects everyone else.

This is an interesting example of a wrong relationship between a wagon and a star, because Springdale is actually not like this at all. As Vidich and Bensman discovered, the class consciousness there is extreme—old aristocrats associating mainly with old aristocrats, professional people with professional people, newcomers with newcomers, shack dwellers with shack dwellers. Once the villagers all got together to repair the dam controlling the stream they all enjoy, but this is one of the few instances on record of community-wide cooperative action. Even the two fire companies are still feuding, fighting fires together but requiring coordination through the office of the regional fire district, a state-supported agency.

There were, by actual count in the mid-1950's, more than two hundred organizations in this village of one thousand, most of them taking only certain people into membership. The only organization open to everyone is the Community Club, formed after World War II by combining several existing local groups, such as the community choir, a dramatic club, and a businessmen's bureau. It now functions through a long list of committees for membership, program, publicity, town affairs, village affairs, school affairs, and community beautification, but its monthly meetings are poorly attended.

Springdalers are fiercely loyal; but why? and to

what? There are no outstanding community achievements to be remembered with pride; no great industries to lend distinction to the place. The school is good, but Springdale shares it with twenty-five other small centers, has no special attachment to it, and values it chiefly as a convenient meeting place. Nowhere does one sense the excitement that bubbles up in a community where people have common concerns and are doing something about them. Apparently the image, the loyalty, and the withdrawal are devices to help the villagers feel more safe and secure in a world that has buffeted their village for more than one hundred years.

There are many good things in their present situation, but, as if to reassure themselves about Springdale, the residents have become harshly critical of neighboring towns and cities. On the other hand, within the village, people do not criticize each other, at least not in public. The only approved outlet for hostile feelings is gossip. Bits of scandal are freely exchanged, always in private and always "in confidence," for public name-calling would destroy the carefully nurtured image of brotherhood. There is general disapproval of three kinds of people: "introverts"—you never know what they're thinking; "bookish types"—they don't keep their feet on the ground; and "intellectuals"—they shouldn't be allowed to get into positions of responsibility.

Under democratic leadership, a village like this might rise above its inner conflicts and parochialism to play a useful part in the development of the area and the state. But the forces that defeat such action in Springdale are strong. The history of this particular place provides no stirring tradition of citizens coming together, setting common goals, working together toward these goals in a far-reaching program of community development. At the present time, there are few channels into the village from the outside along which such cooperative action might be stimulated, because the local professional people—the school superintendent and the teachers, the county agriculture agent, the doctors, lawyers, and ministers—identify themselves more closely with the state and national associations they belong to than with the village, and they do not try to bring these organizations into contact with Springdale's community life.

The village board of supervisors—Springdale's local government—might try for citizen consensus about some local problems, but it has little real power. At the top of the power structure in Springdale at the time of the study were four men who controlled the village through their personal and political influence and wanted no change in the status quo. Under their direction, the board of supervisors handled controversial issues for years by *not* making decisions, *not* taking action in public meetings, and by letting state and national government agencies with local programs take over as many of its responsibilities as they would. For a long time, a local group tried to get authority to raise money for a community center; but the supervisors, prompted by the four behind-the-scenes decision makers, blocked the proposal by ignoring it whenever it came before them, rather than run the risk of increasing local taxes by approving another public facility.

Who can say what the future holds for Springdale, trapped between the past and present by its own inability to take initiative? The exclusiveness, so conspicuous in Springdale's social life today, would be hard to change because it has such deep roots, going back to the time more than a century and a half ago when the village was formed by the union of two hamlets that did not want to come together. Time after time, circumstances beyond the control of the villagers took away their means of livelihood. And with each of these economic shifts came strangers so different from the local people that only a supreme effort on the part of the old residents could have made the newcomers feel welcome and at home. No such effort was ever made.

At present, one of the most hopeful signs for a more

positive approach to life in Springdale is the response Springdalers make when their pride is hurt. Then the whole village rises up in anger. Someday, it may be that under the right circumstances these people will respond to another kind of challenge with equal energy. A sudden awareness of a common need or an exciting opportunity might bring villagers out of their little communities to do something together about a common concern. Then Springdale would really be a community, with all the possibilities real communities have for continuing growth.

RESTON | Preplanned Utopia

Entirely different from Haddonfield and Springdale is a town in northern Virginia that has no past, no traditions, and no fear of social change. This is Reston, a ready-made Utopia, carefully planned, newly built, and claiming to offer a perfect physical environment for the health and happiness of the people of all ages who will make their homes there. Some twenty developments like it are now completed or under construction in different parts of the United States, most of them in California. They represent a trend among city planners and real estate companies to build "ideal" villages and towns, in the belief that these are the logical answer to problems of urban slums, suburban overcrowding, and rural isolation.

The first residents are already settled in Reston, which by 1980 will cover almost 7,000 acres and house about 75,000 people in seven separate villages. The advantages offered are many: Instead of the dull rows of skyscraper apartments one sees in so many housing projects, the houses in Reston are clustered in relation to the landscape, each village with its own garden plots, meadows, lakes, and groves of trees. The roads carry traffic away from the homes, and walks are pathways through woods. There are convenient arrangements for every usual kind of recreation: bridle paths for horseback riding, picnic places, children's playgrounds, and golf courses. A 30-acre lake is already stocked with fish and has a beach for bathing.

Each of the seven villages within Reston will have a mixture of row houses and individual homes. Each village will have its own service area, including a neighborhood drugstore and grocery, but the main shopping place will be the Town Center, where facilities will be available for every kind of entertainment, from a rathskeller for teen-agers to a concert hall. Here, a graceful fifteen-story apartment building is already occupied.

Many residents will commute from Reston to their work in Washington, D. C., 18 miles away, but eventually many will be employed in the community at one of the industries intending to locate in Reston's specially designed industrial park. Only industries likely to employ men and women who will want to live in Reston are being invited to come there. Robert E. Simon, Jr., the creator of this town, believes that people should be able to work near their homes so that the time they would otherwise spend commuting can be used in pleasanter and more profitable ways. In fact, the community is so planned that one can live his entire life in it if he wishes. "You can grow up in one of the houses," Simon explains, "live a bachelor's life in the high-rise apartment, switch to a row house when you marry, and move back to a [larger] house when the children arrive."

If this is Utopia, it has its rules. The soda fountain in the drug store, for example, may have only six seats. Anyone wanting to chop down a tree more than four inches in diameter on his own lot must get permission from the resident forester. Whether he rents or owns a row house, the occupant cannot make any changes on the front of his dwelling without first submitting his proposal to the project's architectural review board.

As time goes on, it will be interesting to see who wins in such ready-made cities, towns, and villages—the people or the management. For the human factor may be stronger, in these developments, than all the preplanning and all the rules of order that go with the finished product. Home ownership is a goal for most Americans, whether the home is a unit in a cooperative apartment building, a cottage in a working-class district, or a mansion on a hilltop in San Francisco. Once they own their own homes, families take pride not only in their houses but in the communities where they have chosen to live. Moreover, homeowners also become very conscious of property rights, especially the right to do what they like with their own places, provided they do not interfere with the rights of others. Millions of American families spend long evenings planning for changes in their homes to be made "when we can afford it," such as a new porch, an enclosed garage instead of an open carport, or a workroom where father and son will have proper space for their tools. Many people even prefer to buy old houses for the fun of remodeling them to suit their tastes. How will Americans, whose attitudes toward their homes and communities are essentially independent and creative, adjust to life in villages and towns already finished for them, subject to stringent planner-builder-management regulations?

Communities with real vitality become stronger, just as families do, in the process of cooperative planning, building, rebuilding, and planning again. Ever-watchful civic groups work through their elected representatives on town and city councils, taking stands for and against proposals to improve the community by changing zoning laws, altering building codes, imposing curfews on teenagers, planting flowering trees along the streets. In towns like Reston, however, residents have no such control over their community life. Each project will probably have a community council made up of residents, but there will be many basic issues this council will have no power to handle. Such groups may be asked to coordinate programs of art, music, and adult education organized in the different centers within a project, but the resident forester will still decide what trees shall be planted or cut down, and the architectural review board may still say "No" to the homeowner who wants to put another window in the front of his row house.

Perhaps city planners like Robert E. Simon, Jr., are right when they assume that a good physical environment is all that people need to make them happy. It will be strange if this turns out to be so. The whole American tradition is against it. For American communities normally develop from within, growing and changing as the people who shape them deepen their understanding of human needs and values. The community now to be described is an unusually good example of how this process works.

ARLINGTON | Years of Problem-Solving

About 180,000 people live in Arlington County, Virginia, a suburb of Washington, D.C., directly across the Potomac River. This is a community where residents display a high degree of initiative and skill in solving community problems. It first gained a national reputation in the early 1940's when its citizens rose in wrath to denounce a bad school system and got themselves a good one in one of the most successful fights for better schools in the history of American education.

In 1940, Arlington was a sleepy place with a scattered population of approximately 57,000. Then came World War II. Hundreds of people came to Washington to take government jobs and crossed the river to live on the Virginia side. Trouble started when these newcomers began looking for schools for their children and were shocked by what they found. Classrooms were overcrowded, children in the first two grades were going to school in double shifts, buildings were run-down, washrooms were unsanitary, there were no proper lunchrooms, and teachers were underpaid. The school board was controlled by a group of local politicians known as "the courthouse gang." In office for thirty years, the school superintendent was sure of his political support and saw no reason for doing anything to change existing conditions. The system was running smoothly, he claimed, at minimum cost to the taxpayers.

At first, parents went to school board meetings—supposedly open to the public—expecting to be heard. They soon discovered, however, that they were not welcome. Members of the school board were appointed by the county board and considered themselves answerable only to that body, which was against any school improvements that would cost money.

Through sheer persistence, a committee of parents finally got a hearing with the county board and requested the supervisors to raise the money needed for the schools by arranging for the sale of county bonds to the public. The county board did not refuse but adopted delaying tactics. The parents were told that they would have to present a petition with 1,000 signatures before their proposal could be considered. The parents countered by forming a Citizens' Committee for School Improvement (CCSI), which included everyone in the county who wanted to join. This committee returned to the county board with a petition for the bond issue signed, not by 1,000, but by 5,000 persons.

The county board maneuvered again. According to Virginia law, the board must now submit the proposal for the sale of bonds to the people of the county at a special election. The board waited a year before calling this election, and then so worded the question on the ballot—prepared and distributed in advance—that very few people could understand it.

The CCSI met this challenge by going to the people

of the county before the election to explain the tricks in the ballot and the need for the bond issue. Members enlisted the aid of press and radio, put up posters, and made hundreds of telephone calls and house-to-house visits. Ten thousand people voted, the largest number ever to come out for a special election in Arlington history up to that time. The bond issue passed, but in a form that provided far less than the sum needed for the schools, and it restricted new building to one elementary school.

The citizens' committee was now convinced that little could be done for the Arlington schools as long as the current members of the school board remained in office. It persuaded the Virginia State Legislature to pass a bill permitting the people of Arlington to elect their school trustees. When the time came for the election of a new school board, the CCSI nominated its own list of qualified candidates to run against the candidates proposed by "the courthouse gang." All five CCSI nominees won on a platform calling for specific school improvements, continuing study of school needs and problems, and a school board responsible to the people of the county. The school superintendent resigned, and an experienced school administrator was found to take his place, a man who held modern views on education and also had a gift for getting along with people. Under this new leadership, the Arlington schools improved rapidly.

The next test of strength between citizens and politicians came when the schools needed still more money and asked for another election to approve a second bond issue. This time the politicians won; the issue was defeated at the polls. Alarmed by the loss of this election, the citizens' committee went to work again, built back its membership (which had lapsed after the initial victory), and gave strong support to the new regime. By 1951, school improvements included seven new school buildings, seven additions to old buildings, new services to crippled, partially blind and otherwise handicapped children, and trained supervisors for music, physical education, and health programs. Relations between parents and teachers were excellent.

In 1954, the county lost the right to elect the members of its school board because of something that happened outside of the county. For 1954 was the year the United States Supreme Court ruled that all American public schools must be opened to Negro as well as white children "with all deliberate speed." Most Arlingtonians welcomed this decision and made preparations to comply with it. But other counties in Virginia were not ready for this, and tension mounted over the integration issue.

Apparently feeling that the counties of the state might work together more smoothly on this and other matters of educational policy if there were a uniform procedure for the selection of school trustees, the Virginia State Legislature enacted a law requiring that members of all Virginia school boards must be appointed by a local governing or judicial body, and specified the method of appointment for each type of school district. In counties with a county-manager form of government —and this includes Arlington—school board members are again chosen by county boards of supervisors, but with many more safeguards than in the past. Fortunately, the political climate of Arlington has changed so much in the last twenty-five years that Arlington residents are generally satisfied with this arrangement, and the relations between the county board, the school board, and the parents are good.

Since the struggle over the schools in the 1940's, Arlington people have made constant use of what they learned then about community organization. In 1954, to keep local issues in focus and the public correctly informed about them, a group of men and women representing business, industry, and the professions organized a forum of civic leaders, The Committee of 100. Community affairs are discussed at the monthly meetings of this group, and if The Committee of 100 feels that action should be taken with respect to a problem, members do what is necessary as individuals or volunteer to report the sense of the meeting to a community agency that attends to the matter.

A particularly interesting program to counteract a growing threat to community solidarity has been under way for the past five years. In the early 1960's twenty-five thousand new people a year were moving into Arlington but not into the Arlington community. These new residents fell into two main groups, those who lived and worked in Arlington, and those who commuted between homes in Arlington and offices in Washington. Newcomers and old residents alike were tending more and more to lead separate lives, not because their interests conflicted, as in the struggle for better schools in the 1940's, but because nothing was being done to bring them together.

County leaders began to work intensively on this problem in the winter of 1962-1963. The Chamber of Commerce sponsored a color film about Arlington to visualize for newcomers some of the special opportunities for pleasant living the county affords. A "town and gown" committee, formed by the Mother Superior of a local Roman Catholic college and a prominent businessman, worked out a scheme for a series of seminars in which newcomers and old residents could study their community together. Hundreds of people and at least seventy-five community organizations participate in these seminars, which have become an annual event. At each seminar, there is an attractive exhibit of the work of both public and private agencies. County officials attend to mingle with the people and answer questions about county government. High school and college students give a great deal of help to this project, promoting the seminars throughout the county in advance and taking part in the programs as speakers and entertainers. This brings the younger generation into the total community effort for newcomer assimilation and gives the students new confidence in their own ability to participate in community affairs.

In 1964, a permanent Arlington Citizens' Participation Council was formed at a meeting of heads of local public and private organizations and agencies, government officials, and other civic leaders. The purpose of the council is "to get more people who reside in Arlington, whether for a brief time or a span of years, to identify with Arlington, to think of it as home, to understand it, and to give time and talent to making Arlington a better place to live, and to enhance the effectiveness of the many Arlington organizations that share that objective."[7] Among the activities of the council are a year-round plan for visits to new families, worked out with the churches, and a program for training neighborhood leaders, led by a specialist from a state university. The county manager expects to have a similar training program for top people in county government. The Arlington men and women who work on these and other projects have only one ultimate goal: to make their community as good a place to live in as they can possibly imagine. They have learned that freedom to create the kind of community they want is never won in a single battle and then possessed forever. They know that they have to protect their gains as they make them and be constantly ready to make new efforts to extend these advances. They also know that they have always at hand three powerful weapons to use if anything should threaten the basic democratic values that motivate everything they do: the ballot box, the courts, and firm citizen action.

[7] From a brochure prepared for public distribution by the council.

V Communities at Work

In 1950, American radio audiences heard a series of broadcasts, called *The People Act,*[1] that is still regarded as one of radio's great achievements. These broadcasts were vivid descriptions of activities initiated and carried on by citizens to solve community problems or to enrich community life. The stories were told so convincingly that the response from listeners was overwhelming; so overwhelming that the broadcasters had to employ a staff to answer inquiries about ways in which communities could start cooperative action or solve problems of community organization. Secondary schools, colleges, universities, and community groups obtained copies of the scripts to use as illustrative material in sociology classes and community discussion groups. Even now, recordings of these scripts are in demand.

Behind *The People Act* was a man with a conviction,

---

[1] Elmore M. McKee, *The People Act: Stories of How Americans Are Coming Together To Deal With Their Community Problems* (New York: Harper & Brothers, 1955). Out of print.

Elmore McKee, a former Yale University chaplain. As a member of the American Friends Service Committee (a Quaker service organization), McKee had gone to Germany at the close of World War II to help with community reorganization. Working at Quaker neighborhood centers in Berlin, Frankfurt, and Darmstadt, he saw at close range the crushing human effect of twelve years of Nazi dictatorship. At home, he had served in communities where citizens, on innumerable boards and committees, had taken responsibility for dealing with community issues. In postwar Germany, he found no such community spirit. Individual initiative had been so harshly repressed for so long that people were afraid to think for themselves and gladly left all community decision-making to public authorities, who took this responsibility as a matter of course.

For the first time, McKee fully realized how easily a people can lose the right to govern itself if it does not use that right to build the kind of society that will protect it. Could the United States lose its independence through such carelessness? He was sure that this could not happen as long as the American people believed in the basic principles of democratic action and were making them work in communities—where American democracy has its roots. But he was not sure to what extent these principles were actually being applied in the eighteen thousand villages, towns, counties, and cities of modern America. In how many of these municipalities, McKee wondered, were groups of like-minded people really struggling, as their forefathers had struggled, to give form and substance to the American dream?

Grateful for the experiences that had given him a new and deeper appreciation of the meaning of American democracy, McKee returned to the United States in December, 1947, determined to share with as many other Americans as possible the insights gained abroad, especially his concern about the health of democracy in American communities. His success in getting his message across to the people is a remarkable example of what an individual can accomplish by his own initiative. First, he undertook a cross-country lecture tour to make contact with people in different parts of the country, to feel again the pulse of community life. Wherever he went, he talked about his work overseas, relating it to the American scene and asking, always, about the processes of local community organization.

McKee was both heartened and disappointed by what he saw and heard on his trip. He met many people with a strong sense of civic responsibility; yet he heard others say, "I'm too busy to take part in civic affairs," or "What can I do? I'm just one among thousands." He found, as he had feared, that in some places "the garments of democracy were becoming shopworn from much handling and too little wearing." But more important to him were the communities he discovered where citizens were handling difficult local problems with initiative and skill. If the strong communities could tell their stories to the nation, citizens who were neglecting their opportunities might be inspired to try similar methods of cooperative problem-solving. The result could mean strengthening and extending the practices of democracy throughout the country.

Radio seemed a natural medium for this new kind of public education. Friends of McKee at the National Broadcasting Company and at the Twentieth Century Fund were able to interest the directors of both organizations in a plan for jointly sponsoring and supporting a series of broadcasts, each featuring a story of a successful community program or project. McKee was commissioned to find the communities. The most talented professionals in the radio business were engaged to write, produce, narrate, and promote *The People Act*. The first series of thirteen programs broadcast in 1950 was followed by a second series of thirteen in 1951, made possible this time by the Fund for Adult Education, one of the independent agencies of the Ford Foundation. The

Columbia Broadcasting System offered its facilities for rebroadcasting all twenty-six programs the next year.

To realize as fully as possible the potentialities for civic education in the broadcasts, a National Committee for *The People Act* was created in 1951, with Milton S. Eisenhower, then president of Pennsylvania State University, as its chairman. A campus building became *The People Act* center, where a staff handled letters, telegrams, telephone calls, and visits from more than 10,000 persons during the active life of the program (1950–1953).

In 1955, McKee published eleven of these broadcast documentaries (expanded and updated) in *The People Act*. In his preface, he points out that although it begins with the story of a radio program, the book becomes the story of a cooperative movement involving great numbers of Americans eager to demonstrate that local communities are, indeed, the testing grounds of a free society. One of the stories dramatized for the broadcasts and included in the book is told again here—how Tin Top, a Texas settlement, lost and recovered its sense of community. The other stories in this chapter came from friends working on the projects or familiar with them for other reasons.

TIN TOP | Rebirth of a Community

About the time that Texas became a state (1845), pioneers heading south came to the rich bottomlands and grassy uplands of the Brazos River, in the north central part of the state, and settled there. By 1850, some thirty-three families had settled on both sides of the river, in an area some 54 miles square, a little to the south and west of the present city of Fort Worth. They built their log cabins on holdings of from 100 to 5,000 acres and started their farms and cattle ranches.

Cotton was the first crop. It paid so well that the cotton farmers could soon afford to build themselves a community cotton gin—a device for separating the seeds of the cotton plant from the fibers. The gin was housed in a shed with a galvanized iron roof that gleamed in the sunlight and could be seen for miles on a clear day. "Look," the ranchers would say, "Tin Top is showing up." And by this name the settlement came to be known.

In the early 1900's, Tin Top still consisted of thirty-three scattered families, most of whom managed the farms and ranches of absentee owners. Tin Top could not be called a hamlet, much less a village, but it *was* a community. The thirty-three families had common interests and worked together to meet their needs, as the building of the cotton gin showed. Families visited each other as often as they could, but homes were far apart, and farm work kept everybody busy from morning to night. The tiny trading center contained the gin, a small store, two churches of different denominations, and an outdoor tabernacle for religious revival meetings. Major shopping was done by mail or in the town of Weatherford, about 10 miles away. The children attended a one-room school at Balch, a nearby settlement.

In 1920, the women of Tin Top formed a Home Demonstration Club[2] to study better ways of managing their homes and caring for their children. Anything that these wives and mothers could learn that would lighten their work must have been a blessing, for the homesteads had no electricity, no running water, no indoor bathrooms. The women did the housework and cared for their families under the most primitive conditions. In addition, they milked the cows, churned the butter, and helped in the fields. In spite of the hardships, however, life in the community was friendly and good.

---

[2] Home Demonstration Clubs are part of a nationwide program of adult education for homemakers. They are sponsored in each state by the state university with assistance from the United States Department of Agriculture. The overall program is known as the Cooperative Extension Service of the United States Department of Agriculture.

Early in 1930 the world turned upside down for Tin Top. Crop-eating insects, the worldwide economic depression, and a long drought put an end to cotton growing in the region, and the gin was sold. The churches closed and the Home Demonstration Club discontinued meetings, chiefly because transportation was too hard to arrange. The store remained open but had almost nothing to sell. The little school at Balch was abandoned in a statewide program of school consolidation, and the youngsters were sent by bus to larger schools in neighboring towns. This contact with town life excited the older children, who began to look beyond Tin Top for recreation. Even the parents were seeking entertainment away from home, combining shopping with ball games and movies when they could get to town. Tin Top, as a community, seemed about to die.

Community spirit, however, lives or dies in human beings, not in land or buildings. So even when it seems to be gone, there is often a spark that can be rekindled. This is what happened when Grace and Bickham Cartwright were married and came to Tin Top to live on the 800-acre ranch they owned there. They were saddened by the deterioration they saw around them and began looking for ways to help the people of Tin Top recapture their old community spirit.

One day in the fall of 1947, the Cartwrights stopped their car beside the two closed, shabby churches. Suddenly Grace turned to her husband.

"Bickham," she said, "let's paint the churches."

"We might try it," Cartwright said thoughtfully. "We might try it."

The local preacher gave his permission; the Cartwrights sent over some of their ranch hands with the paint and came themselves to help put it on. Soon the two buildings were once more clean and white.

That simple but important effort rekindled the people. The Home Demonstration Club met again and voted to reorganize. It also voted to call a community mass meeting to decide about something special that had come up. The *Farmer-Stockman*, a national farm magazine, had announced a community improvement contest, with a first prize of $1,000. If Tin Top wanted to compete, it could, in so doing, make some of the local improvements that were badly needed anyway.

Fifty people turned out on a night in January, 1948, to discuss the contest. They voted unanimously to enter it and immediately chose a committee to manage their participation. This committee listed the areas of major local need, appointed a steering committee to take executive responsibility, and set up a number of subcommittees to explore and work on problems in each area of need. Everyone in Tin Top of school age or over was put on one of these committees.

During the ensuing year, these committees worked hard, with amazing results. With the help of the Rural Electrification Administration of the federal government, the electricity committee got power lines extended into Tin Top, so farm families now had electric lamps to work and read by at night, electric pumps for their wells, power tools for their workshops, and laborsaving electrical appliances—vacuum cleaners, electric irons, and washing machines. The clean-up committee weeded the churchyards and got twenty-two farmers to bring their axes and cut away the thick brush obstructing the road to the bridge over the river. The church committee brought lunches and spent days scrubbing and repainting the insides of the churches. The teen-age committee built a baseball diamond and did what it could to help the other task forces. The recreation committee organized some small but successful social activities; it even experimented with dramatic performances. A game committee worked with state agencies on wildlife conservation and on plans for stocking farm ponds to provide fresh fish for Tin Top families.

These achievements were the substance of the report entered in the *Farmer-Stockman* contest. Meanwhile, Tin Top had been officially incorporated as a political entity, with a mayor (Mrs. Cartwright) and an elected community council. "With all the work and play and worship together during the first year of organization," Grace Cartwright wrote to a friend, "we began to feel a sense of belonging again. Roots were going deep, we were no longer isolated families, yet something was missing. The young people were leaving the community. Why?" Efforts to answer this question led to the biggest project of all, the building of a community center in 1949–1950.

All during 1948, the recreation committee had struggled to "make do" with the inadequate facilities available for games, dramatics, social evenings, and indoor sports; now it was discouraged. Until Tin Top had a place where people could meet, play, and work comfortably together, really good community entertainment was impossible. The steering committee of the community council held many long discussions about this problem with people in and out of the community, trying to find a solution for it. The answer finally came when one of their consultants, an absentee landowner, suggested, "Let's build a community center and make it a memorial for Lonnie and Bryant," two boys from Tin Top who had died in World War II. The suggestion delighted the community, and plans for the project started to crystallize immediately. Lonnie's father gave the land. The community council donated $100, and with this much in hand, the center was incorporated as "a voluntary association to support undertakings for the benefit of the community in general."

Following the same pattern of organization used in preparing for the contest, a steering committee soon had everybody helping. One committee cleared the brush off the site, another wrote to Texas A & M College for designs for the building, and still another wrote to several civic theater groups, asking for suggestions about building the stage. The designer of the famous Shamrock Hotel in Houston, Texas, Wyatt Hedrick, became very much interested in the project and drew the blueprints for the building, free of charge.

Stones from the ranches and other materials were hauled to the site in pickup trucks when men could spare time from their farm duties. Steel was donated by a nonresident landowner. Surveyors working nearby offered to dig a well. A farmer in a neighboring community gave cement and sent his own men to pour the floors for the building and patio. The kitchen equipment came as a gift from a vocational school in Weatherford. A high school in a nearby town gave lumber. The floors were laid by Tin Top men, who also built the porches, two stages, and a terrace. The women helped with everything but took special responsibility for the landscaping.

To the housewarming on February 19, 1950, came families from all over Tin Top with gifts of dishes, chairs, chests, linens, a gas stove, and even a used piano. Tin Top now had a beautiful community center, made of native stone and paid for with the original $100 from the community council, $7,000 raised or donated by individuals and groups, and thousands of hours of labor contributed voluntarily by Tin Top families and their friends.

One of the first big celebrations in the new center was a dinner in honor of Sam Whitlaw, editor of the *Farmer-Stockman,* who had come to award Tin Top second prize of $400 for its entry in the community improvement contest. The people of Tin Top were proud of this recognition, but the contest was already behind them. "What pleased them most," said Robert Trout, a radio commentator who was present, "was not the prize, but the fact that they were a community and were so considered by the judges. They felt they had a past and, more important, a future."

"We were sorry to see the meeting end," Trout said later, when he narrated the story of Tin Top in *The People Act* radio series. "We drove back down the lonely country road, in the pitch dark, but suddenly it didn't seem lonely any more here, in these 54 square miles of Texas, where thirty-three families got together and became a community."

That is what happened in Tin Top. Some of the projects started between 1948 and 1950 eventually came to an end, but others kept springing up. Telephones were installed in 1952. Family solidarity and neighborliness have grown steadily through the years. One of the gayest of the annual celebrations in Tin Top is Homecoming Day, when people who have left the community, especially men in the armed forces, come back for reunions with their families and friends. A supper meeting is held once a month at the center to discuss community affairs. Following an old pioneer custom, each family brings a dish it has prepared to be shared at the meal. After supper, there is a business meeting and entertainment. The money for Tin Top's varied activities comes from both public and private sources and is handled in five separate accounts, all in good shape—an educational fund, a game preserve fund, a cemetery fund, a homecoming fund, and a public utility fund. The community is still managed by a five-member board of citizens and is completely solvent.

People who know Tin Top best have several explanations for the success, in general, of the efforts made there to revitalize the community. They call attention to the timing: When Grace Cartwright suggested repainting the churches, Tin Top was weary of its own dreariness and thankful to be able to do something about it. There was the sharing that went on: All of the thirty-three families in the area helped with the planning and the work. There was the clever way in which Tin Top multiplied its own resources: by calling upon state and federal government agencies for assistance and by giving talented outsiders a chance to contribute.

More important, perhaps, than any of these factors was the wise, imaginative, selfless leadership from 1947 on. One of the men who worked closely with Grace Cartwright through the triumphs and the heartaches of the program paid her the highest compliment a community leader can receive: "We couldn't have started without her," he said, "but we [could now] go on without her." Young people to take the place of older leaders come readily out of a community that has been spiritually as well as physically reborn.

WATERFORD | Village Restoration

Northern Virginia is pleasant country. The wooded hills are low, and in the valleys between are small farms, big estates, orchards, and many little towns. One of the oldest and most picturesque of these is the tiny village of Waterford, in Loudoun County, about 40 miles south of Washington, D. C.

A walk on a weekday afternoon down the main street of this Waterford (there are several other places with the same name in the United States) is a journey into the past. Colonial houses face each other across the tree-shaded road, those on the upper side separated by stone passageways that give glimpses of charming patios built into the hill rising behind. Sidewalks are mostly of brick and cobblestones. It is easy to imagine an eighteenth-century lady in crinoline alighting from her carriage at the entrance to one of the small shops.

Waterford was settled by Quakers about 1740. One of the big houses still standing is known to have been built before 1751. During the Civil War, the village was surrounded by fighting, and the people suffered greatly from prolonged anxiety and lack of food. But the hardest times came with the depression of the 1930's. Between 1930 and 1940, Waterford became a dreary sight. A few of the homes had been bought and repaired by new-comers, but many of the houses were unoccupied. Others looked as if they might fall down at any moment.

The change began when Edward Chamberlin, a wealthy blind man in the community, shared with neighbors and friends his dream of a complete village restoration. With the help of his brother, Leroy Chamberlin, Edward bought one of the oldest and most interesting properties in town, a row of dwellings near the village green. The dwellings were built separately but had been joined together in 1800 and used as a tavern for almost 100 years. Plans for improving this property were well under way when Edward died and the work stopped, to the dismay of many people living in and near Waterford. Unwilling to give up Edward Chamberlin's dream, which by this time had become their dream, too, a handful of local residents met one day in 1943 to consider what they could do to carry on the restoration project. These men and women knew that Williamsburg, the first capital of Virginia, had been rebuilt in the image of the lovely colonial town it once had been. But they also knew that this restoration had cost millions of dollars and that a private foundation had provided most of the money for it.

"Anything as ambitious as the reconstruction of Williamsburg is out of the question here," the friends agreed. "But why can't we do what we want to do in a simpler way?"

This first voluntary planning group made three important decisions: (1) to promote village restoration as a community project involving as many Waterford residents as possible, with the understanding that the main cost of restoration would be borne by individual homeowners responsible for work done on their own places; (2) to form a corporation that would give leadership in the development and coordination of an overall restoration plan and raise funds for certain activities of benefit to all; and (3) to arouse interest in the way of life as well as in the architecture of colonial Waterford.

The first objective was accomplished within five years. By 1948 practically every historically important house in Waterford was in good condition again. Private owners of these dwellings were proud of them, restoring them with taste and elegant simplicity. The simplicity is traditional, for Waterford never was a "stylish" town.

The original, informal planning committee incorporated itself as the Waterford Foundation in 1943. The purpose of the corporation is "to recreate the Town of Waterford as it existed in previous times, with its varying crafts and activities . . . and to restore as many buildings as possible in the Town of Waterford in like manner in which they were originally constructed." A rather unusual pattern of organization has been worked out to provide a good basis for fund-raising: The board of directors is self-perpetuating, and there are three kinds of members—*associate members,* elected by the board and allowed to attend board meetings but not to vote; *sponsor-supporter members,* financial contributors; and *general members,* a small invited group from which new members of the board are chosen. Special committees are appointed as they are needed. For example, a collection committee gathers and mounts (for exhibition purposes) photographs of Waterford buildings before and after rehabilitation.

The foundation carries on two main groups of projects: handcraft and art projects, and the restoration of public buildings. The first money in its treasury came from the purchase and resale of the oldest house in the village. Friends made possible the second real estate transaction, the purchase of the Old Mill in 1944. Besides the Old Mill, the foundation now owns, by deed of gift or purchase, the Red Barn, a smaller barn containing a blacksmith forge, the old stone jail, the old undertaking establishment, the old corner store in the center of the village, and, across the street from the store, the little log house known as the Weaver's Cottage.

The third foundation objective, revival of interest in colonial customs and activities, is achieved mainly through special projects, classes in colonial arts and crafts, and the annual fair. The special projects, such as the sale of an attractive engagement calendar illustrated with Waterford scenes, usually have a specific fund-raising purpose. The classes are organized from time to time during the year to teach pioneer skills (still fun to practice), such as quilting, weaving, hooking and braiding of rugs, candlemaking, and woodworking. Articles made in these classes may be exhibited or sold at the fair.

The fair, officially called the Annual Waterford Homes Tour and Craft Exhibit, is fondly known to most of northern Virginia as the Waterford Fair. On three days in early October each year the village opens its doors to visitors, who come by the thousands from far and near to sightsee and to shop. Twenty-two years ago, the fair began in the living room of one of the old houses with a modest display of such homemade objects as rugs, bedspreads, baskets, and hand-dressed dolls. Today it is such a tremendous undertaking that preparations for the next one are started before the last weary child has been carried away from the current year's marionette show.

The program for each day includes exhibits, demonstrations (potterymaking, for example), visits to a few of the private homes, and entertainment. Home-cooked meals are served in several convenient places about the village by local organizations that make money for their own work in this way. Ladies from the Loudoun County Home Demonstration Clubs, dressed in colonial costumes, usually make apple butter in a huge copper kettle over a wood fire on the village green.

Perhaps the most remarkable thing about the Waterford Fair is the cooperation it has earned from residents of the surrounding countryside. Hundreds of people work for it all year long without remuneration. At fair time, county officials see that the roads leading into Waterford are tidy and in good repair. The school board allows the Loudoun County Parent-Teacher Association to use the school to serve lunch for visitors and lends acres of school land for parking. The county sheriff sends police to direct traffic through the narrow, winding streets of the village. County organizations, such as the Home Demonstration Clubs, the Boy Scouts, the 4-H Clubs, and local church groups help with the work in innumerable ways.

Although the Waterford restoration project would make a nice story for an operetta, it also has a serious side. It shows a carefulness of planning that is sometimes lacking in larger community programs. The Waterford people knew that it would take time to do what they had in mind and that their means were small. They were willing to work slowly and carefully toward their goal, taking advantage of all the help they could get, but never undertaking more than they could afford.

Compared with more ambitious restorations in other places, the Waterford enterprise is a modest undertaking, but it has all the values one hopes to find in a truly creative endeavor. It is a homely venture, warm and intimate and full of meaning, not only for those taking part in it, but for the many who come to enjoy the fair, if only for a day. It taps apparently inexhaustible sources of energy and talent in the people associated with it. Workers and spectators alike gain from it a new sense of history, of belonging to both past and present. Perhaps most important of all, Waterford leaders believe that there is timeless beauty in the arts and skills of colonial village living, and they make it possible for friends and neighbors to reveal this beauty today in the work of their hands.

NORTH PHILADELPHIA | New Approach to an Old Problem

As so often happens in cities that are very big and very old, standards of living vary tremendously in Philadelphia, Pennsylvania. In some parts of town, people live in comfort; in others, poverty is extreme. One of Philadelphia's most worrisome "poverty pockets" is a section of North Philadelphia, where more than a quarter of a million Negro families lead a wretched, hand-to-mouth existence. Most of the houses are sagging, rat-infested tenements. The streets are filled with litter. But the bitter, underlying problem is unemployment. In 1964, approximately twenty thousand Negro men and women of the area were jobless and could not get work. Their frustration was one of the principal causes of race riots there in the summer of that year.

In such a community one would hardly expect to find hope. Yet today in North Philadelphia hundreds of people are radiant because of a project that is already changing their lives. This miracle is a new kind of vocational school where Negro Americans (and white Americans, if they wish) may train, in short practical courses, for a wide variety of jobs in modern businesses and industries, knowing they will be placed in suitable positions when they finish their training.

A ten-minute ride from downtown Philadelphia brings one to the school, housed in a building that looks like, and once was, a police station. Across the front of the building, a banner carries a picture of a key and the words "We help ourselves." Over the entrance is a sign in bold, bright letters: Opportunities Industrialization Center. Even before one enters the place, one senses the enthusiasm of the eager young people hurrying in and out of the front door.

This school, the first of its kind in the world, is part of a seven-year-old effort to solve the unemployment problem in Philadelphia. In the late 1950's, Philadelphians were gravely concerned about two problems in their city: juvenile delinquency and unemployment, especially unemployment among Negro youth. To get at what they believed to be the common underlying cause, a group of Philadelphia citizens organized a Youth Community and Employment Services program in 1958 and placed a vigorous Negro leader, Reverend Leon Howard Sullivan, in charge of it.

By 1961, Reverend Sullivan and his administrative assistant, Reverend Thomas J. Ritter, were both convinced that a placement program, however good, could never solve the problem of Negro unemployment for two reasons: many employers were not willing to hire Negroes, and very few Negroes had the skills or training that would enable them to compete successfully in the labor market. At best, the youth center could place only about one-fifth of its young Negro applicants.

Attacking the first of these two problems, Reverend Sullivan led four hundred ministers and their parishioners in a series of boycotts against a group of Philadelphia businesses and industries known to be using flagrantly discriminatory employment practices. The boycotts opened up three thousand new jobs for Negroes in the Philadelphia area, but this was only a partial victory; there were not enough qualified Negro workers to fill the new positions. There were rumors of coming federal government funds for job training and retraining, but government programs move slowly, and tension in North Philadelphia was mounting rapidly.

"These young people have to have training and they have to have it *now*," the two ministers agreed. "We will set up a training center of our own, and if we have to, we will use volunteers as teachers." "Actually," Reverend Sullivan said later, "we didn't even have a screwdriver to start with, but we knew that somehow we would find a way."

The two leaders called a meeting at Reverend Sullivan's Zion Baptist Church, inserting advertisements in local newspapers asking all employed skilled craftsmen and technicians in the community to attend. They appealed to the three hundred who came to volunteer their time as instructors. The appeal was powerful; practically all of the workers present offered their services. Coincidentally, the mayor of Philadelphia was planning a job training program, and the Philadelphia Chamber of Commerce was working with the local industries, trying to get them together to set up private vocational and technical training schools. When representatives of the mayor and the Chamber of Commerce called on Reverend Sullivan to ask for his cooperation, they learned for the first time what he was trying to do. In the end, they abandoned their plans in order to help him with his.

The search for a location for job training classes ended when an interested member of the Philadelphia City Council arranged for the use of an abandoned police station at a token price of $1.00 a year. This building was in awful condition. Most of the plaster had fallen from the walls, electric wiring hung loose, windows were broken, the plumbing was useless, rooms and hallways were littered with trash. The size of the clean-up job was overwhelming but the families in the neighborhood realized what the center could mean to them and came forward to put the building in shape. Volunteers of all ages went to work sweeping out rubbish, pulling loose plaster off walls, taking out rusty pipes, prying fragments of broken glass out of window frames, scrubbing woodwork, so that plasterers, carpenters, and painters could come in to do their part.

This was a good start, but no one yet knew exactly where the money would come from for the project. Reverend Sullivan applied to a foundation for $6,000 toward the repair of the old police station. A representative of this organization, examining the building carefully, said, "You couldn't put this place in order for $50,000!" The foundation later sent a check for that amount. Equipment for the various vocational shops and classrooms, donated or loaned by local industries, began to arrive—modern machine tools, instruments, all the equipment needed to teach machine tooling, electronics, power sawing, teletyping, sheet metal work, commercial food preparation and service, and chemistry laboratory work. A second foundation gave $200,000 through the Philadelphia Council for Community Advancement. The federal government made two sizable grants, and 1,000 community volunteers raised $102,000—$52,000 from families in the surrounding area and $50,000 from local businessmen. On January 26, 1964, when the Opportunities Industrialization Center, Incorporated, was formally dedicated, 8,000 neighbors and friends jammed the street before the door. These people had every right to be proud, and the words "We did it ourselves" seemed to float like an echo up and down through the crowd.

The center opened with a waiting list of 6,000, but lack of space limited enrollment to 300 persons at a time. During the first year, 500 trainees were graduated, 80 percent of them going immediately into good jobs. Pressure from would-be students and prospective employers forced the center to open two branches before the end of its second year. Department store selling, merchandising, and small business administration are now taught in a six-story office building lent by a Philadelphia businessman. The second branch specializes in training for laundry work, dry cleaning, and the building trades.

All courses are adjusted to meet the individual needs of trainees. Some of the units are short and some are long, depending on the skills to be mastered. For example, the center trained five sheet-metal workers in a special process in ten days for a company manufacturing school furniture. A vocational counseling service helps the trainees to choose the work they are best fitted for and then develops employment opportunities for them. The fact that jobs are waiting is a powerful incentive to young workers who once saw no benefit in further education.

In 1964–1965, the center's budget for the year was approximately $300,000. At the present rate of expansion, the annual cost will probably stabilize around $2,000,000. This may seem like a large sum until one realizes that the city now spends more than $100,000,000 a year on Negro welfare. Every recipient of relief who becomes a wage earner not only reduces the welfare budget by a considerable amount, but he also adds the skills and self-confidence he has newly acquired to the total economic potential of the community. Residents of North Philadelphia have just completed another $100,000 drive, industry has promised to continue its support, and the government has increased its contribution so that the center can train 4,000 young men and women in 1966–1967. The instructors are now receiving salaries that compare favorably with salaries paid teachers in similar positions in industry or the regular vocational schools. A few teachers still give their services without charge.

Soon after classes began, the teachers found that they had a bigger problem to deal with than mere lack of vocational skill. Most of the young people they were working with were so undereducated that they had trouble understanding what was said to them and even greater difficulty expressing themselves. They had never learned to speak clearly or to take messages or to use the telephone in a businesslike way. They did not know how to apply for a job or how to behave in order to keep one. For the leaders of the center, this discovery was a challenge. To provide basic education for the thousands on the center's waiting list, Reverend Sullivan and Reverend Ritter organized what they call a "feeder program." This includes classes in simple reading, writing, and arithmetic, emphasizing the vocabularies and the mathematical concepts future workers will use on their jobs. In addition, there is instruction designed to help young people make the very most of their personal assets —lessons, lectures, and demonstrations on health and personal grooming, wise buying, and good manners.

When they are ready for the shift, students from the feeder program are guided into vacancies in the center, or into other appropriate vocational training programs, and also into public school adult education courses. Some are soon ready for full-time jobs as clerks, receptionists, and maintenance workers; a few go on into government service.

Exceptionally well qualified teachers are sought for this massive training effort, and the newest teaching equipment is being used—closed circuit television, movie projectors, tape recorders, and so forth. Distinguished Negroes, including Dr. Ralph Bunche of the United Nations, Jackie Robinson, the baseball player, and Marian Anderson, the singer (herself a native of Philadelphia), are on the list of guest speakers. For Reverend Sullivan believes that meeting successful Negroes will help the young Negroes of North Philadelphia develop a more optimistic sense of the possibilities for themselves as American citizens. "You don't have to spend the rest of your lives on handouts and welfare," he told a class recently. "You are part of an historic demonstration, and upon your performance will depend the futures of 20 million persons in our big cities who have been brainwashed into thinking they are inferior. But I tell you the Negro is not inferior, and genius is color blind!"[3]

The response to this program has been phenomenal, showing the hunger in the community for education that begins where the learner is and takes him where he wants to go. The first feeder program had a quick enrollment of 750; 250 more had to be turned away for lack of room. The first classes were held in the unused community building of an old synagogue. Fire recently destroyed this building, but the governor of Pennsylvania immediately offered the temporary use of the National Guard Armory. Neighborhood centers are being organized as rapidly as possible.

Through the feeder program, a constant search goes on for individuals with leadership potential who can be trained for work in other community youth programs and community organizations in North Philadelphia and elsewhere. Their work will be in building community action study programs in their own and other neighborhoods. The entire effort is thus focused on

---

[3] Quoted from an article, "Toward Self-Help in Philadelphia," by Paul Friggens in collaboration with *Reader's Digest*, published in *The Christian Science Monitor*, September 15, 1965.

helping people in local communities gain sufficient pride and self-confidence to continue to help themselves.

"Good Hope Corner," as the Opportunities Industrialization Center is often called, is a busy, vital place. The center has been licensed by the State of Pennsylvania as a private vocational training school. There will be further financial assistance from the government, but this is simply regarded as "just income from another source"; in accepting it, the center has not given up any of its independence. The thousands of neighbors who helped to create it can still say, "This is ours. We did it ourselves." However, this experiment has more than local significance now because the federal government has given it a place in the vigorous campaign initiated by President Johnson to eliminate one of the main causes of poverty in the United States—unemployment. The North Philadelphia leaders have been sent about the country by the federal government's Office of Economic Opportunity to advise with people in other communities wishing to set up similar local job training programs. By the summer of 1967, sixty-six of these had been established.

People who have studied the North Philadelphia program say that much of its success is due to remarkable leadership. But there are other reasons why it has gone so well and so far. Again, as in Tin Top, the timing was right. Negroes without work in North Philadelphia were desperate. Everyone in the city in a position of responsibility knew that something had to be done to help them. Furthermore, in the neighborhoods where unemployment was highest, there were men and women with understanding, common sense, imagination, and the ability to think about possible solutions in terms that were big enough to match the size of the problems with which their neighborhoods were faced. With labor, industry, the city, state, and federal governments, and the citizens most concerned united behind the plan, the resources and the power represented by this combination are tremendous.

The Opportunities Industrialization Center may be a temporary solution to one aspect of the problem of unemployment, an intermediate step toward a new kind of vocational education organized to meet the needs of the new age of technology. But the "feeder program" is different. This is a social invention, a new kind of adult education that can open the door to opportunity for thousands who need basic education in order to grasp the job training opportunities provided by vocational training centers, or who simply want more general education for personal reasons. This door can stay open as long as there are people who want to go through it. The success of the entire experiment shows again how generously and how joyously a community will rise to support action that meets deeply felt community needs.

GUADALUPE | An Awakening

The flowering of our forty-eighth state is an exciting and colorful story. Within the short space of one hundred years, Arizona's scattered little towns became cities; her mines yielded treasures of gold, copper, silver, and other precious minerals; great irrigation systems brought water that released the fertility hidden in her arid soil; industries developed to process her ores and crops; her health-giving climate and the grandeur of her scenery attracted visitors from all over the world.

Left behind in this surge of prosperity was the sunbaked little Arizona town of Guadalupe, where until very recently six thousand Indians have led wretched lives, isolated from the rest of their busy English-speaking state by barriers of language and poverty, alienated from each other by old tribal jealousies and fears. Even those who found work in Tempe, five miles away, never felt themselves part of the mainstream of American life.

Guadalupe was settled in 1910 by Yaqui Indians who fled across the border from Mexico to escape religious persecution. They were a proud and industrious people, agriculturists with a genius for military organization, but nothing in their history had prepared them to cope with the conditions they found in Arizona. They could not farm the desert land without water, and they had no capital to begin irrigation on a big enough scale to ensure an adequate living. They became gaunt with hunger and dreamlike in their movements through lack of energy and hope.

As poor as the Yaquis, were the American Indians who joined and soon outnumbered them. If the two groups had been friends they might have solved some of their problems by working together, but their mutual suspicion kept them in constant conflict. Even when Arizona became a state in 1912, their feelings toward each other did not change. They were all Americans now, but so far removed from the developing political life of the state that citizenship meant little to them. In the early 1960's, Guadalupe and its people seemed to have reached the depths of despair.

The outlook for the town in the spring of 1964 was disheartening. The streets were still unpaved, there was no police or fire protection, no public health service, no place for the children to play except the dusty main street, the equally dusty plaza, or the forbidden irrigation ditches on the big commercial ranches that now encircled the town. The main street was a death trap for young and old alike because there were no traffic signs or other means of traffic control. During the hottest weather, town water was often turned off to conserve the supply; water carried from the ditches against orders frequently brought sickness; sickness, in turn, brought more misery because of the lack of medical care. If patients from Guadalupe had to be taken to the overcrowded hospitals in Tempe and Phoenix, they felt lonelier and more unwanted than ever, for the doctors and nurses did not understand their language and seemed to be too busy to sense their needs.

When the bus from Guadalupe to Tempe was discontinued, the town faced utter disaster. Guadalupeans who worked in Tempe no longer had a way of getting there, and the loss of their jobs meant further hardship for their families. The only available work at home was in the fields at very low pay. In order to buy the necessities of life, people went deeper and deeper into debt at the local stores and withdrew more and more from contact with each other. Sometimes one postman can create a feeling of neighborliness as he carries the mail from door to door, but Guadalupe did not even have home mail delivery. Travelers in the cars that sped through town must often have said, "What a dead place! How lazy the people here must be. They don't even care enough to clean up the yards around the houses where they sit."

But there were people in Arizona who understood what was happening to Guadalupe and did not consider the situation hopeless. Representatives of the Presbyterian Church of the United States knew about Guadalupe; they also knew a man named Fred Ross who seemed to have a remarkable ability to help people help themselves. Ross was a member of the staff of the Industrial Areas Foundation of Chicago. At the time, he was serving as a consultant with the Community Services Organization of Mexican Americans in California. At the request of the Presbyterian Church, the foundation assigned Ross to Guadalupe, the church organization paying his salary.

What Fred Ross found when he came to Guadalupe was more discouraging than he expected. There was human energy there, but much of it was being wasted in the traditional friction between American and Mexican-American Indians. There was little contact with the school. To most parents, this building was a frightening place where they went only if their children were in trouble. After more than fifty years of citizenship, Guadalupeans still had no interest in politics or voting. They believed that politicians would take their votes and then forget them.

But there were at least two bright spots in the local picture. A priest had persuaded two public health nurses in Tempe to volunteer their services in Guadalupe to run a family health clinic. These women were coming out from Tempe two evenings a week, after their regular day's work was over, to do what they could for the sick people who crowded the little room used for an office. And there was a local Indian of Yaqui descent, Lauro Garcia, who had the kind of executive and leadership abilities that had once enabled his ancestors to play an important role in Mexican history.

Ross took Garcia into his confidence and then went to work in his own way. At first, it was hard for anyone but Lauro Garcia to see what Ross was doing, because he just seemed to be talking with anyone who would stop and talk with him. But because he was talking with townspeople about *their* problems and *their* feelings, he stimulated them to continue the discussions with each other. Soon, one of the Indians said he thought they might have more influence with persons in a position to help them if they banded together. So a community association was formed in which Mexican-American and American Indians both participated. This was called the Guadalupe Organization, soon known simply as GO.

The first GO project was an effort to show the people of the town why it was important for them to register for elections and to vote. This campaign was highly successful. More than seven hundred residents of Guadalupe registered in the early days of the drive, and in the 1964 elections Guadalupe had not only a higher proportion of residents voting than any other town in the county, but the second highest in the state. The wisdom of this approach to community improvement was soon apparent. Buttressed by the newly developed voting power, delegations from GO carried their most urgent problems to the appropriate county, state, and federal government authorities for action, requesting police and fire protection, playgrounds for the children, classes in simple reading and arithmetic for adults, traffic control within the town. The GO representatives got positive action almost overnight. The mere mention of seven hundred new voters was enough to command the immediate attention of elected officials.

Within three months, the progress made was almost unbelievable. The highway through the town had ceased to be a death trap, for the county furnished twenty-five stop signs, and GO members put them up, enforcing the speed limits as well as they could until the county assigned a police officer to Guadalupe. Two miles of town streets were surfaced, at a cost of $10,000 to the county. A playground was built for the children. Five public school classes in reading, writing, and arithmetic were started for their parents. A doctor was obtained for the health clinic; he now comes regularly once a week from Tempe with a registered nurse.

All of this activity started in April, 1964, spurred by the presence and imagination of Fred Ross. At the end of five months, Ross had to leave, but by this time Guadalupe knew how to act on its own behalf. By the end of October, 1964, a local man had been hired by the county sheriff's department as the town's first full-time police officer, and door-to-door mail delivery was provided by the United States Postmaster General. A special clinic for babies had been added to the health center. A new, efficient water system was installed in the town. Garcia, trained by Ross, ably took Ross's place.

As people in Guadalupe talked and worked together, they learned how to proceed in an orderly way to eliminate the problems that had once defeated them. They learned about the different government agencies and private organizations available to help solve the kinds of problems they faced. They learned how to approach these agencies, how to state their needs, and how to get the help they sought. When the leaders of GO heard the federal government was creating a program to help poor communities with advice and grants of money, under the Economic Opportunities Act, they learned how to apply for a share of these funds. Later, officials in Washington, D.C. said that the proposal from Guadalupe was the second best received from any community in the country. Now Guadalupe is requesting assistance in job training and retraining from the Federal Office of Manpower, Automation, and Training. Now, too, a special effort is being made to encourage high school graduates to continue their education in colleges or technical schools, with the aid of scholarships for qualified candidates.

The most recent news from Guadalupe is as exciting as the earlier reports. GO has set up a credit union to encourage saving and help people pay off their debts. Arrangements have been made for the doctor and two nurses to come twice a week to the clinic. The application for funds to the Federal Office of Economic Opportunity has been granted: $67,000 has been allotted to GO for its work. The Roman Catholic Bishop of Arizona has given GO $5,000 for the same purpose—an example of interfaith cooperation between the Catholic Church and the Presbyterians who started the Guadalupe community program.

In Guadalupe, the seemingly impossible was accomplished in an amazingly short time in the simplest possible way—by getting people who had distrusted each other for years to talk together long enough to discover their mutual interests and common concerns. Breaking the barrier of noncommunication was the first big contribution Fred Ross made. Once over this hurdle, he could show the people of Guadalupe how to define their problems and encourage them to discuss solutions.

From that point on, the usual steps in the problem-solving process were applicable—plans were formulated, accepted or rejected by the groups involved, tested in action and, if necessary, changed. Ross was the catalyst. He asked questions, offered suggestions, taught procedures, and made official connections where local citizens could not. *But he exercised no authority, and he never took away from the people he was working with the right to make their own decisions.* He knew that no one really understands what citizenship means until he has had some part, however small, in community decision-making. The citizens of Guadalupe are now ready to be active participants in the further development of the thriving and colorful state to which they now feel they belong.

The descriptions of community programs and projects in this chapter are success stories. Perhaps stories of failing communities should have been included to balance the picture. For there are many places in the United States where the patterns of local community organizations are more authoritarian or laissez faire than democratic.

But it is not really important that some towns have not yet achieved community status. The struggle for growth and survival is always going on somewhere, and there will always be American communities in every stage of development. As Elmore McKee points out in his book, *The People Act,* communities that have become organic wholes are "the signatures of a people who mean to stay free." And in an open society their examples are contagious. At one time or another, workers in every successful community program are asked for advice by workers in other places who want to try new ways of solving their own community problems.

Since every community in the United States has its own individuality and is in some way different from all the others, it is pertinent to ask: To what extent are successful community programs transferable? Never entirely, of course. The ideas that work in one town or neighborhood may not work in another. But all flourishing community programs have some characteristics in common: They are all built by volunteers who are willing to work hard, without pay, for the good of the community as a whole. Leadership comes, eventually, from within the community. Steps are taken early to assure community understanding and support. Opportunities are provided for all concerned to participate in program development, in the making and evaluating of decisions, and in a variety of worthwhile, cooperative activities.

As programs grow, the number of people taking part in them increases. Generally, these people trust and respect each other and avoid the formation of cliques. Channels of communication within a program are kept open; information and ideas are freely exchanged, in and out of meetings. It is taken for granted that citizens will respond when they feel that the challenge is real. Every task is approached in a spirit of inquiry: What is the problem? What are the facts? Are more facts needed? If so, how can they best be obtained? What are some possible solutions? Which of these should be tried first? What human and material resources are available? What are the possible sources of financial support?

American community organization is not a panacea for every social ailment nor a pattern for social action in every country. Every society has its own dynamics and must find its own ways of working out its destiny. Still, there is a universality in the philosophy underlying American community development procedures. That is why the stories in the radio series *The People Act* were rebroadcast by the Voice of America and the Armed Forces Network to audiences around the world. The People Act Center on the campus of the Pennsylvania State University received requests for copies of the scripts and for more information about the communities from Alaska, Hawaii, Canada, the Philippines, Japan, Korea, Great Britain, Germany, Austria, Africa, Israel, and India.

An American soldier from Tin Top wrote his parents, "I was flying over Iwo Jima heading for Korea. Someone turned the radio dial and we got the Voice of America broadcast of the Tin Top story. Gosh, can you imagine how I felt, as we went on to Korea to add to the destruction of the last raids, to get the story of you folks building things up?"

A United Nations command officer in Korea sent for the script of one of the stories and had it translated into Korean and Chinese for prisoners of war, who staged the broadcast as a play. He said, "It tells, through Americans who participate in community action, what America *is*."

VI The Meaning of Membership in a Community

One of the most essential things about any community is how membership in it is established: Were its people born into it or did they choose to live in and be a part of it? Were they forced to live in this certain place or are they there because they did not know of any other kind of community to join?

The United States is thought of as a nation that was chosen from the beginning by its citizens. So the idea of American community contains many of the memories of the earliest self-chosen groups—the little bands of pioneers, adventurous spirits, or members of a fleeing religious sect—who formed themselves into communities and, by so doing, had the right to decide who else could live among them.

As the country opened up, settlement was freer than anywhere else in the world. There were easy provisions for homesteading land, and people clustered together for many different reasons; but the old idea persisted that the members of each small settlement had, somehow, the right to determine who lived there. So two rights persisted: the right to move, by any route and any kind of transportation, anywhere in the United States, without a passport or a "by-your-leave," as long as you had money to pay your way; and the right of a group of people to decide what sort of people were going to live in their town. There is a curious contradiction in these two ideas, but they both go back to actual conditions in the first two centuries of the existence of the United States. For a very long time, these ideas applied only to the colonists themselves, not to slaves or the descendants of slaves or to American Indians or their descendants. If an inn had a room and the traveler had the money to pay for it, the room should be his. There were only a few cases of actual class-divided types of travel in the United States, and these depended solely on money. Those who had enough money could buy a sleeping berth on a train or a boat; those who did not, could not. Anybody might move in tomorrow, from anywhere, and if the town was new enough and rough enough, like the old frontier towns of the West, with just a hotel and bar where cattlemen and lumbermen came on Saturday nights, people did not ask questions of the stranger.

But as soon as the town became a real town, with families living in it, a town with a school and a post office, a general store and a church or so, then the welcome to any stranger became more cautious. He was welcome only as long as he behaved himself. If he did not behave himself, the same thing might happen to him that happened to the ship's captain in the poem, "Skipper Ireson's Ride," by John Greenleaf Whittier.

> Old Floyd Ireson, for his hard heart,
> Tarred and feathered and carried in a cart
> By the women of Marblehead!

This was not done very often, but the more backward and isolated the town and the less the people in it had been exposed to people with different skin color and different habits, the greater the likelihood that strangers and dissenters would be forcibly run out of town.

Even in the original colonies, running people forcibly out of town was outside the law. The law gave a man freedom to live and move within the colony, and later, within the United States. It protected his right to move, protected him from bandits and highwaymen, prevented other men from obstructing his movements. Later, as the power of the central government increased, all sorts of reforms were introduced in the statutes that applied whenever people or property crossed state lines. The United States government, in its relations with its citizens, deals with individuals, with organizations of individuals, and with agencies of state and local governments. Unless a federal law is broken, the federal government leaves to the states the regulation of everything that happens within a state and the right to deal with each individual. But at the local level, in the village, or town, or suburb, groups still form that seek to set up their own rules of behavior, supporting or opposing other people, not as individuals but as members of other groups of which they do or do not approve.

So these two conflicting ideas—the idea that every individual should be free to come and go as he pleases, build any kind of house he likes on his own land; and the idea that people have a right to choose their neighbors, with whose children their children are to play, and to regulate what kind of houses those neighbors can build—have been the basis of conflict in the United States from the beginning.

Some small colonial settlements banished people for religious beliefs or bad behavior; others, like the little colony of Rhode Island, prided themselves on welcoming those whom less tolerant communities had expelled. There is a colorful story of two adventurers who came to Plymouth to make trouble for the colonists. Although they were so plainly guilty that more direct action might have been taken, they were given the benefit of a full and proper trial, attended by everyone in the settlement.

They were sentenced to leave the colony, but even so, justice was tempered with mercy. Their wives and children were allowed to stay until the men could "remove them comfortably." Town dwellers who feel that their communities are especially desirable have always been nervous for fear too many, or too many of the wrong people, would move in. Yet the freedom to move, to buy property, to do what you liked with your own house, no matter how much in so doing you might spoil another man's view, was also a fundamental right.

The problem of what to do with the indigents who move from state to state is older than the United States itself. In 1758, the New Jersey Provincial Legislature passed an *Act for the Settlement and Relief of the Poor*, for the purpose of restricting immigration from other colonies and the movement of vagrants, "so that each county and township would not be responsible for the support of any except its own poor."

These fears and hopes were embodied later in the so-called settlement laws of other states, laws that required each newcomer to be a resident of a state for a certain length of time before that state would be responsible for him. They also specified how long he could be away from the state looking for work and still be eligible for public assistance if he came back unemployed or ill. When the local poor relief laws were translated into nationwide public welfare legislation under the Social Security Act of 1935, the states retained the right to set up their own settlement laws (more often called, now, "residence requirements"), but these must be somewhere within the limits set by the federal Social Security Act, since every state now receives part of its welfare funds from the federal government. During World War II, some of the states were very much afraid of being overwhelmed by newcomers and stiffened their residence requirements. California, for example, had a waiting period of three years. Rhode Island, on the other hand, remained true to the spirit of earlier days. Though crowded with defense industries and recent migrants, Rhode Island proudly abolished all settlement laws.

As the United States developed into a settled nation with a large population, there was less interest in bringing in foreign workers. Entrance into the country and the right to hold government jobs and other public offices became more restricted. From 1922 on, immigration laws began to reflect American prejudices. Laws were passed in which future immigrants who were expected to look most like the idealized earlier settlers—those from the United Kingdom or from western or northern Europe— were given preference over immigrants from southern Europe. There were restrictions on Asian immigration and on the immigration of people from the Caribbean and from Mexico.

For a long time, the United States had thought of itself as a nation in which the poor of Europe were welcome, a nation which had inscribed on a statue at her main port of entry the words:

> Give me your tired, your poor,
> Your huddled masses yearning to breathe free,
> The wretched refuse of your teeming shore.
> Send these, the homeless, tempest-tost to me,
> I lift my lamp beside the golden door!

Between the two world wars the picture changed to become one of a United States besieged by those who, fleeing from political oppression at home, thronged American consulates all over the world.

Again there was the conflict: Everyone should be allowed to come, but the people already here should choose who could come. Just because so many Americans feel very strongly about freedom of movement, conflicts over immigration to the United States have always been sharp. Feelings run high, and the rest of the world comes to participate in the quarrel. The harder it is to get in, the more the newcomers, fleeing from concentration camps, refugee camps, and starvation, value getting in. Once accepted, they, in turn, insist that all those who are here are here because they chose to come. "If you don't like it here," they say to the discontented, "why don't you go back where you came from?"

But given the choice, it has been almost inconceivable to most Americans that anyone would choose not to be an American. The recent exodus of young men to Canada to avoid the draft is unprecedented. The few well-known Americans who have elected to live in Europe and give up their citizenship are objects of wonder, for there is almost no tradition of virtuous rebellion against the American government. Americans feel that the American Revolution was not fought against its own government but against another country ruled by a foreign king. America's government was chosen by self-elected Americans. As it has self-correcting features and belongs to them, Americans feel they can change it when they wish; therefore, there is no need for either secret or open rebellion against the government. Those who do not like it can go somewhere else to find or form another kind of government, just as the colonists did when they came here.

The Civil War, in which the right to leave became not just the privilege of the individual but was claimed by a group of eleven states, cut across this belief in free choice. The North denied, enforced by arms, the right of the South to secede from the Union and so, in southern feeling, turned the conquered South into a sort of colony of the North. Defeated, the South felt trapped in a position in which there was no choice at all. Southerners loved their land, their states, their own way of life, and they turned fiercely to remembering the ways of the past. Political conflicts between North and South continue to mirror this bitterness, but the Union has endured.

Other parts of the former colonial world took a different course. South and Central America were divided into many small states. Today, the peoples of Africa have also taken a different course, as splinter group after splinter group has been able to break away both from colonizing countries and from ineffective federation.

The inability of Americans to understand someone who voluntarily gives up his American citizenship, or would risk giving it up, lies back of the feeling that all radical attempts to alter the American form of government are un-American and foreign. The idea of treason in the United States is the theme of the famous late nineteenth-century story, *The Man Without a Country.*[1]

These conflicts between the rights of those who first chose to come and the rights of others who chose to come later are still reflected at the community level in two principal areas, housing and schools. Towns try to regulate residence by zoning laws prescribing the kind and cost of the houses that can be built in certain areas. Sometimes these restrictions are so extreme that schoolteachers, for example, cannot afford to live in the towns where they teach, if these have only large houses and blocks of flats are not allowed. From such zoned towns, those who have owned houses may have to move when they retire because there are no smaller accommodations for the aged and infirm. So these become towns for people with good incomes and large families only.

The original definition of membership in American communities was based both on choice and on ownership of property—property acquired by an individual either because he belonged to a company that had received or purchased the right to a given piece of land, or because one of the agencies that had the right to the land had sold or assigned it to him. In early Connecticut towns, those whose means permitted them to make the largest initial investments in the community received the most desirable house sites in the center of the town, while those who could invest the least were given plots of land on the periphery. In turn, it was the people on the periphery, with the lowest stake in the community, who were the first to move.

---

[1] Edward Everett Hale, *The Man Without a Country.* First published in the *Atlantic Monthly,* December, 1863.

Giving the men with the largest stakes the largest voice was in many ways an equalitarian idea. After all, it was they who had put the most into the community and were quite justifiably most concerned with it. The largest voice did not depend on rank or position, only upon the amount invested. It gave position, rather than proceeding from position, and the position it gave was local. The fact that a man was a large property owner in one town or in one state gave him no rights whatsoever in another town or another state. Over time, those who stayed and prospered in any community became dominant in its affairs. A certain number of failures settled down in the poorer sections; and a large number of individuals pulled out to go elsewhere, usually farther west, and later, into larger cities. Newcomers in a town had to demonstrate their right to participate in the town's affairs by living there a certain length of time and, ideally, by owning property and so paying local taxes.

Except for special licenses, most local taxes are real estate taxes, and local responsibility was and is tied to ownership of real property—land and houses. It is the owner of a house who pays the taxes and is responsible for seeing that his tenants obey town ordinances, such as keeping up the sidewalks in front of their building. If the snow is not cleared away within a given number of hours after it falls on a walk, the owner of the property is subject to a fine. Should a stranger slip on ice in front of a house or on the steps, or anywhere on a property, the house owner is liable for damages. This law has been extended to the automobile, which in many ways is now a moving house rather than simply a vehicle to get from one place to another. The owner of the car is responsible if his vehicle injures someone else or damages property that does not belong to him.

Congruently, in many communities, only those who can own land and buildings have a stake in what happens; the citizen's suit against government injustice or undue interference is, in local affairs, a property owner's suit.

In big cities the owners of large blocks of houses, not the tenants, are the responsible persons, as taxpayers, and subject to regulations. As an extension of owning property, a local voting residence also became a condition that had to be met before one could be an effective member of the nation. Today property ownership still validates the owner's right to participate in the affairs of his village, county, town, or city, but guarantees him little more than this.

Poll taxes were eliminated mainly because they were used as a way of disenfranchising a very poor section of the population. But residence in a given locality for a given length of time is everywhere a requirement for voting, and even soldiers overseas receive their ballots in terms of their local residence. People who travel far or move often may not vote for many years because they cannot fulfill the requirements of living a certain number of days in a ward or a town and a certain number of months in a state. Number of years in the United States is still the principal criterion for citizenship, coupled with a minimal knowledge of the principles of American law and government. So while property gives individuals a higher stake in their villages, towns, and parts of cities, either residence or membership in the armed forces determines the right of citizens to vote in local, state, and national elections.

And in almost every settlement in the United States, those who have lived there longest and owned real estate are regarded as having better standing than those who have lived there without owning real estate, or who have just recently arrived. In any town, the earlier residents, from whatever ethnic group, tend to have a greater prestige than the groups who came later. Thus one ethnic group will be dominant in one town, and a different ethnic group in another. In New England, long-time resident and property-owning Negro Americans will be treated as citizens deserving more respect than recent immigrants from southern Europe. In some small towns,

Jewish citizens may be treated as members of an aristocracy based on early settlement; in others, they may be the poorest of newcomers, doing factory work.

Furthermore, status in one town or one part of the country does not confer status in another. In the Old Southeast there was a considerable emphasis upon ties of kinship, and these grew even stronger after the Civil War, so that genealogical relationship became more important there than ownership of property or education and occupation. But in most parts of the United States, a family's standing is determined by the position its members hold in a given town, and this cannot be taken with them if they move, except in terms of very personal ties to people in the new town. As a man becomes more prosperous, he may buy a house in another part of a large city, move to another suburb or, if his present position is very conspicuously different from the position in which he was born, he may even move a long way from his city of birth and make a fresh start. Initially, in a new place, he and his family will be judged by the house and the particular part of town they live in. If their behavior fails to live up to the house, they may be isolated and rejected. Children in high school and elementary school may be accepted more easily by local residents than their elders.

Because so much depends upon where a man lives, most community problems center about questions of housing and residency. There have been, and still are, long battles over the right of any group of residents to keep members of other groups whom they consider to be undesirable from owning property or living in a given town, suburb, or part of a city. Such restrictive attempts vary according to region. The restriction might be the posting of signs warning members of some minority group to be "out of town by sundown." They may be efforts to control residence in a neighborhood by zoning regulations about the size of the lot and the cost of a house that can be built on it, supported by individual restrictions on buyers that prevent them from reselling to members of unwanted groups. There is even an occasional private and elegant small town with gates and guards protecting people of a given income and style of life. Selling an apartment in a cooperatively-owned apartment house requires the approval of other owners.

Within restricted living areas, people not only assume great responsibility for upholding community values, but also feel that they are protecting their children, assuring them of association with children of comparable status who will catch the same kinds of diseases, use the same words at play, and grow up with a uniform style of manners. At present the most extreme expression of this attempt to provide a protected and uniform environment for one's children is the one-class suburb, where all the thousands of residents, regardless of their ethnic origins, pay about the same amount for their houses. They may represent one or several ethnic and religious groups. The important thing now, however, is their attempt to attain a uniform standard of living for their children.

The conflicts over rights to community membership sometimes focus on attempts to pass laws that make it compulsory for anyone to sell his house to any would-be purchaser. Restrictions on buying into any village or housing development or apartment building are experienced as affronts to human dignity by members of minority groups who are refused admission on that account. Because of the sharpness of the affront, the laws that are drawn up to combat such restrictions tend to be coercive. Fair housing laws may have a variety of paradoxical clauses, such as a requirement that the owner sell to the highest bidder, which would, in practice, force the minority group member to pay a higher price for living in a given neighborhood than do members of the majority group.

Along with this American attitude towards the house and grounds as the basis of rights and responsibilities goes the attitude toward those who rent rather than own, and toward all transients. Although about one-fifth of the American people now move every year, and the right to move is so important, renters and tenants are, nevertheless, commonly treated as irresponsible individuals. Sharecroppers in the South, both Negro and white, are expected to be always in debt, within a system organized so that they would always be in debt. This attitude toward the transient and the renter is often reciprocated by carelessness and near-vandalism in hotels and bus stations and by irresponsibility toward the owners of the rented houses and flats. And this whole complex of attitudes lies behind the tremendous premium upon owning your own home. A house is called a home before it is even purchased by its first owner. In 1960, 56 percent of American families owned their own homes; 38 percent rented the places where they lived.

Some so-called home ownership is, in fact, a legal fiction. A man may own a house by making a small down payment; sometimes even this is not required. He pays the rest of the cost in the form of a mortgage, usually financed by a bank, often through a government loan. His monthly payments on the house may be less than the rent he would have to pay for a house of the same kind, so by "owning" the house, his monthly cost for shelter may be considered a form of saving. If he leaves town for a better job or is transferred to another job somewhere else, he can sell his house for the amount that he has now invested in it and so "buy" a new house in the new community. This should, theoretically, give him a great deal of freedom, but it frequently results in a considerable amount of failure and unhappiness. If for some reason a town suddenly loses a factory or industry on which it has depended, if a military base closes down or an airplane factory is discontinued or the mine ceases to yield any more gold, silver, or coal, if the oil wells give out or farm crops in the area on which the town depends suddenly go down in value, a man may find himself owning a house he cannot sell. This can tie him to a town where he can no longer find profitable work.

When such things happen, people in older American settlements, as in so many English towns in the 1920's and 1930's, sometimes settle down to a life of despair and indigence, living on in the only places they have ever known, even when the only work they have ever known has disappeared. When this happens, people may feel frustrated and unhappy. Somehow their expectation that owning a house is a way of being free has turned against them and, instead, a house becomes a liability. Under these conditions, they may become bitter and angry against vague powers like "Washington," or some "they" whom they hold responsible. Two towns with very much the same kinds of people in them, one of which is growing and offering new work opportunities while the other has shrinking work opportunities, may vary widely in their political attitudes.

Over time, in particular towns, one man or a group of men or a big company may come to overshadow all the rest of the homeowners as employer, landowner, tax-payer, and initiator or blocker of community action. Sometimes this huge power is used beneficently, but such power is, on the whole, disapproved of. Ideally, a town should have a variety of different interests that balance each other.

Just as attitudes toward housing and residence reflect traditional American attitudes toward freedom of movement and freedom to choose one's close neighbors, so attitudes toward the schools reflect the conflict between freedom and equality. In colonial days, there were community, elementary, semipublic schools, plus a smaller number of secondary schools that prepared a selected few for a life of higher social status than their fellows. Academies for boys and finishing schools for girls came into being early. Thomas Jefferson worked hard for a state system of public education for all children in Virginia, but his plan was defeated in 1779. In the settled seaboard states, private schools developed side by side with systems of public education organized under pressure from early labor organizations, like the Knights of Labor. The emphasis on free public education was increased by concern for the children of immigrant groups in the cities. If these children were to have a chance in the new country, they had to be taught the rudiments of how to live in it. Public education was definitely a system that was fought for in the name of the underprivileged, supported by privileged people who were both broadminded and philanthropic. It was also something that the entrenched members of society were asked to provide for the poor, the uneducated, and the immigrant newcomers.

However, the model of the public school was the little red schoolhouse where everybody, from the banker's daughter to the child of the poorest farmhand, went to the same school and sat side by side. But as cities grew, a pattern in which public schools were used to differentiate instead of to unify began to emerge. The first suburbs appeared, and it was possible for a group of people of the same kind to have a public school system exclusively for their own children. Such schools are nominally equalitarian, but actually they are strongholds of special privilege.

In order to improve the poorer schools, funds and standard-setting had to come from larger units—from the great city, from the state government, from the federal government. Poor towns, slum areas, areas of new, barely assimilated immigrants could not provide either the money or the leadership needed. And so some state control and state subsidy of the public schools came into being. Education became compulsory, first for little children, and then, slowly, for older boys and girls. As the number of years of compulsory schooling increased, high school became a possibility for every American child, and today we are struggling to produce a system where higher education (junior college and college level)

will be available for everyone who domonstrates a capacity to benefit from it.

Meanwhile, the schools—who goes to them, who
teaches in them, and what books are used in them—
remain a central concern in every American town and
city. In spite of state funds and state laws and heavy subsidies for special purposes from the federal government,
the American school system is still a decentralized
system, with some thirteen thousand independent school
districts in the country. These districts have little in
common except their autonomy. The controlling group
may be rich or poor, old inhabitants or new immigrants.
The district itself may be a slum, with residents who
have had little formal schooling, a suburb where the
lowest income is $30,000 a year, an abandoned mill town
where nearly everyone is on relief, or a scattered farming settlement.

The struggle for a good single public school system,
a system combining local responsibility and control with
help from state and federal government agencies and,
sometimes, from private foundations, epitomizes most
of the other struggles in American life. A city decays at
the center if all the young, educated, responsible parents
move, for their children's sake, out to the suburbs. A town
or city falls apart if what parents want for their own
children and what they want for the children of the
whole community are somehow separated and discrepant.
If the property owners are too alienated from the families whose children go to school, there will be difficulty
in passing bond issues to build new school buildings. If
the wealthy people in the town send their children to
private schools, responsibility for education will be
divided. If the town grows overnight from 1,200 to 10,-
000, as some American towns do in periods of sudden
prosperity, the schools will be hopelessly overcrowded.
Children will have to go to school in shifts, and a tremendous effort will be needed to get any sort of adequate
education program going. If there are large religious

groups who send their children to parochial schools, there may be trouble in getting the necessary funds to improve the public schools. If there are strong political differences in the town, these may be focused in the schools, in a quarrel, for example, over what should be taught about the United Nations or a United Nations special agency, such as UNESCO or UNICEF. Each new shift in American aims and purposes is reflected in the schools.

It is hard for peoples whose schools are controlled by central, governmental authorities to understand the vivid participation of American parents in what goes on in the local school—over such issues, for example, as how mathematics is taught, or what slogans are to be used in teaching history. Whereas in most other societies issues of this sort are decided either by the central government or by the educational directors of large regions, in the United States they are primarily matters for local concern. In 1916, a reform mayor in New York City lost his bid for reelection because immigrant mothers rioted against a new system of specialized teaching that forced their children to walk up and down many flights of stairs during a school day. How the teachers teach, what the teachers think, what they read, and how they behave have always been matters of concern to American communities.

In many parts of the world, university students take an active political role. In the United States, university students have been relatively inactive politically; usually only small groups become involved with social and political issues. It is not as students, who are not yet full members of the society, but as young parents of children who must be educated to live in that society that Americans become actively involved in the political process.

It is when they must choose what kind of neighborhood they want for their children now and what kind of schools, what kind of town planning, what kind of future they want for the country, that Americans come to realize the great amount of choice there is in the United States. Except for the chronic slum dweller and rural poor who are tied to land that is no longer productive and have neither the outlook, the means, nor the energy to leave, every American always has before him the opportunity to choose whether he will stay where he is, on this street, in this part of town, or leave this street, this part of town, this city, altogether. Will he go where it will be better for the children, or stay where he is? Such choices are widest in times of economic depression, when people have nothing to lose by moving, and in times of great prosperity, when it is easy to move. In 1949–1950, when the country had just about settled down again after World War II, 25,551,000 Americans moved into different homes. This was about one-sixth of the whole population at that time or, put in another way, more than the total present population of Norway, Sweden, Denmark, and Belgium. Most of those who moved were in search of better conditions, and by "better conditions" they meant, primarily, better conditions for their children, a better or safer place for young children to play, and better schools for the older children.

At the same time, it is essentially the responsibilty of the people who do not move, or at least have not moved this year, to keep the community going, to see that it is not disorganized by the flood of newcomers, and that the newcomers themselves are involved in any necessary changes. A school system may end a year with twice as many children as it had at the beginning. In some Florida winter resort towns the schools open with a low enrollment which doubles and trebles in the winter months and decreases again in the spring when people, both the vacationers and the people who work to make vacations pleasant, go home again. In many parts of the country new housing developments are run up almost overnight; hundreds of families move in, lawns still a morass of mud, streets partly laid, but children all ready for school.

Many of these moving parents, although looking for services that local communities can provide, are essentially unrelated to the local community. They are likely to be the ones who are in favor of more state aid for, and control of, the schools, and they may protest against local bond issues.

So, increasingly, the mobile, the poor, and the dispossessed look to larger, more impersonal agencies to provide the services needed for their children. Families who move would like to have a more uniform school system, nationwide, so that their children could go from school to school without losing a year here and there because of differences in the manner and the content of the teaching. Families who move would like to have uniform requirements for such things as automobile insurance, so that they would not have to go through different sets of legal procedures in different states. Families who move would like to have nationwide regulations about how the trash is put out, and whether you can or cannot mix paper and tin cans, or paper and garbage in garbage containers.

But families that stay, families who have lived for generations in the same place, cherish the way they have always done things, are proud of the way they have got along together, are "set in their ways," and are not anxious to have newcomers come in demanding that things be done differently. And one of the ways in which old inhabitants temper the eagerness and fresh energy of newcomers is to give them the most difficult jobs. For example, there is a new, very active woman, with four children in school, who wants to play a role in the Parent-Teacher Association. Very well, let her. Make her chairman of the program committee, or make her chairman of a committee to try to get two neighboring primary schools to do things together; *that* has been tried and failed at least ten times. She'll learn!

Fortunately, the newcomer with extra energy and a desire to make the schools better for her children, very often goes ahead and succeeds where others have failed. She arranges to keep the school building open every weekday night, or to have special, supervised play on Saturdays. She gets a lot done before she learns how difficult it generally is in that particular town to get *anything* done. In fact, American community life depends upon the ebb and flow, not only of life itself, but of such coming and going. People fret about someone who is a genuine obstacle to progress—say, a man who has been superintendent of schools too long, or a chairman of a library committee who has held the post for so many years he thinks he owns both the job and the library. Then some wise older person says to the impatient junior, "But remember, people do die or move away." And in the United States, oftener than in most nations in the world, they do move, if not out of town, at least out of one organization into another, and other people move in.

A town in which there were no newcomers would, in time, be very static, stirred to activity only by some catastrophe or by some major event that would bring in a spate of newcomers. For active community life, a town needs to be growing, but not too fast, and it needs a reason for new people to come. New industries opening up and providing new jobs, permanent institutions of the kind that have high turnover, such as colleges and universities, scientific laboratories, research institutes: these are the things that give a town personality and style, that bring in new blood, and give assurance that among the newcomers there will be people with talent.

When all the children go to the public school, and housing is not so arranged that the schools for little children, built near their homes, reflect only one ethnic group or one economic class, the school provides a place where the new child can bring new experiences to the others—the taste of a new cookie, new games, new ways of counting out to see who will be "it" in a game. Just as parent newcomers provide stimulation to the complacent older organizations, so their children provide stimulation to the younger ones. It may be hard on a child to move, to leave his former friends and playmates, the tree that he has just learned to climb, and enter a strange classroom filled with thirty staring pairs of eyes. But in situations like this, American children learn poise, learn to speak in front of others, and learn to establish friendly relations quickly. These are skills that will be needed later.

In providing a model of the whole democratic process, the schools both succeed and fall short. A free public education for every child is the American ideal. Actually, in many parts of the country, parents with unusual children (children with greater talent than the average child, or children who are physically or mentally handicapped in some way), parents who are ambitious for their children to enter a very good college, and parents who have ideas about education that the local school board resists (such as teaching a foreign language in the primary school, or having more handicrafts or some form of the new mathematics) will send their children to private schools. In many parts of the country, all children do go to public schools, but this is not necessarily a hardship. Some suburbs have public school systems as famous as the old, named schools of England, and instead of paying high tuition for private schools, parents will often buy houses in these communities, even though the taxes may be very high.

The Roman Catholic Church has always maintained separate schools where much of the teaching is done by teaching orders, and the families of children who attend pay some tuition. To some people, this seems unfair; for if the parents are property owners, they are paying a school tax for schools their children do not attend. In the case of some minority groups—Asians on the Pacific Coast, Mexicans in parts of the Southwest, Negro Americans in the Southeast and in cities in the North where there are large Negro populations—many of the best suburbs are inaccessible because of private real estate agreements that keep minority groups out. So the recent national legislation and agitation for open occupancy is really legislation to make it possible for all parents to choose where they want their children to go to school. And here, again, is the belief in the right to move and to challenge the customs and values of the people who are already there, trying to defend themselves against too many strangers.

So, many people turn to legislation to protect the freedoms that they feel are threatened. Some concerned people fight for wider legislation to provide for fair housing, better housing, more colleges, better mental hospitals, and better "halfway" houses, places where people who have been mentally ill can live in a semi-sheltered environment until they are ready to come back into the community. Concerned individuals fight for changes in laws on birth registration so the birth certificates children take to school will not show whether they were born in or out of wedlock. Obviously, if such laws can be made national laws, then a greater victory appears to have been won, and the rights of individuals, whether newly born innocent children or people who visibly have African and Asian ancestors, are protected everywhere. If a national law isn't feasible—and often it is not, because the problem in question is within the jurisdiction of the states—then those defending and extending the rights of individuals will try for state laws. All such laws, whether state or national, make it easier for the advocates of some form of more democratic behavior to work for it in their own communities.

But there will be those who wish to defend some form of life that they already have, to keep their community a pleasant little town of substantial homeowners of the same race or class or religion. They fight against big housing developments filled with strangers who, unused to living in suburbs and small towns, may spoil the trim appearance of their tree-lined, flower-bordered streets. The old inhabitants will try to protect their rights by working for local ordinances, such as zoning laws, or by seeking to locate the next high school so as to separate the children of the "better" class of people from the others. Or they may give up altogether and start private schools or send their children away to school.

Still, when the public conscience is aroused by signs of too much privilege, there will again be an attempt to correct the imbalance. Active and interested citizens at the local level will protest, and some may even demand that children be taken long distances in school buses to overcome the inequities that have arisen from housing restrictions that make one disadvantaged group cluster in one part of a town. These worries will also be felt in the private schools. Some of their supporters and parents will demand that they be diversified by economic class or race or religion, or they will look for a certain number of pupils of foreign origin. This, in turn, will be still more expensive for the parents who, as property owners, are already paying school taxes for public schools to which they don't feel they can send their children. Diversifying a private school means providing scholarships and money to pay for the underprivileged pupils.

In other parts of the country, parents set up private schools because the public schools have become little tyrannies where individual parents, or even groups of parents, have no power to protest. The administrators of a school system may decide not to prepare any child to enter a college more difficult than the state university, which is often required to accept any student who has finished a secondary school in that state. Teachers may become so certain of their methods that parents are "forbidden" to teach their children to read before they enter school or to help with their homework. The school system may have a policy of promoting children with their age mates, no matter how unready they are to go ahead; or a state may pass a law that no child is to stay in one grade more than two years. So pupils are placed in classrooms where they themselves cannot learn and where they interfere with the learning of other children. Some youngsters in both groups will become truants and delinquents, the retarded through despair as they drop further behind, the gifted through boredom as the work gets progressively easier and less challenging. Yet the answer here is not for educated parents to take their children out of school and teach them themselves, because under the law they may be legally prosecuted for doing that.

So the parents, if they must live in such communities, have no redress. They can, if they are sufficiently public spirited, join some organization fighting to change these laws, or they can persuade other organizations to which they belong to fight for change. But what good is that going to do the four-year-old, sitting on the floor begging to be taught to read, when you know it is against school policy to admit any child under five? "He'll be in high school before we can get the law changed." So if the dissatisfied parents can find other like-minded parents with time and energy for the task, they start a private school, a school that will express all the new ideas of the moment and give their children now—before laws can be passed, reforms introduced, new curricula written—the education the parents think their children ought to have.

But so strong is the pressure against exclusiveness that no sooner have these parents started their new school, doing most of the work on it themselves, often contributing more time and money than they can afford, than they again begin worrying about what the role of a private school should be. True, it should be experimental; it should be able to do things, or at least try things, that a public school cannot; but it shouldn't be restricted only to fortunate children. There should be scholarships and more scholarships, and the school, started for a few, struggles to move to create opportunities for the many.

This struggle, between people whose goal is a first-class, tax-supported public school system and those who want to use private funds to establish private systems that will be qualitatively better and almost necessarily more exclusive, is representative of struggles that go on in many other sectors of American life. Having no available private school—that is, no choice for the parents of a child who does not fit into the public school except to move away—seems intolerable. But when private schools multiply until the time and energy and interest of most of the substantial people in a town or of a dominant religious minority group are diverted to them, and improvements for the public schools get fewer and fewer, the result is a bad public school system for part of a city's children and isolation for the group from which responsible leadership in the next generation is most likely to come.

So people who have already moved from a crowded urban area where they could not stand the school conditions—overcrowding, old dilapidated buildings, poorly trained teachers, noise, and dirt, and the aggression that poverty and deprivation bring—will move again, in desperation, to a beautiful, exclusive suburb. Here they find that their children meet no children who are poor, no strangers except a couple of children whose fathers are diplomats. They begin to worry about the narrowness of their children's lives, and work on schemes to get their children back into the city where they can meet and talk with children of different backgrounds!

And in times of very rapid change—as in the present push for civil rights in the United States—federal law may have to be invoked (because of the tremendous diversity of sentiment in different parts of the country) to reduce the concentrations in ghetto-like neighborhoods, and to disallow laws that separate children classed as Negro from children classed as white in both the South and the North. Then the feeling of the dispossessed, newly hopeful of obtaining their rights, and of those of the majority group who have deeply identified with the plight of the minority, rises high; and there are demonstrations, strikes, and sit-ins to compel a reorganization that will include children of all groups within the same school.

And so the struggle goes on to make a democratic community with immigrants from every part of the world participating; to reconcile the dreams of the first colonists and the inequalities new settlers bring with them; to preserve freedom of choice and yet give equal opportunity to all. And the principal burden falls upon local communities, where battles may be won or lost, depending on the presence or absence of alert and watchful leaders. The price of liberty is eternal vigilance.

VII Patterns of Community Action

Every society has its own ways of getting things done—ways of providing the services it needs, ways of acting in emergencies. Sometimes, when people move from one environment to another or from one country to another, they may be helpless, feeling that they have left behind some essential part of their past—the priest, perhaps, or the wise man to whom they turned for advice or legal decisions, or the rich man who protected the poor, or even the money lender. As people from all over the world came to the United States, they came as individuals or individual families, and rather quickly learned American patterns of action; or they came in groups, with a sense of mutual support that enabled them, sometimes, to keep their own ways for a very long time. Sometimes, if there were enough of them, they left a permanent stamp on the part of the country in which they settled.

American patterns of action came originally from northern and western Europe and the United Kingdom and have much in common with the rest of the English-speaking world. American children learn these patterns when they are very small; the first struggles may occur on the playground over who is to be president of a new club. The patterns are repeated in youth clubs, in church meetings, at the business meetings of all sorts of associations; the rules recur in the minutes that are read, and in reports in newspapers. That these organizational things are done differently in other countries surprises visiting Americans as much as do strange foods and different mealtimes. It is almost as if they believed that the rules of parliamentary procedure were part of some sacred scripture, delivered from on high in the morning of the world.

The pattern by which American organizations are started and carried on is essentially the same, whether the purpose of the founders is to do good, to enjoy each other, to work for some legal reform, to support each other professionally, to perpetuate a common past, to start a church, to found a joint stock company, or to launch a new political party. Children, adolescents, responsible businessmen, worried young mothers, old ladies, owners of cats, parents of retarded children, former alcoholics, stamp collectors, any handful of people with mutual interests, may constitute themselves a club, a society, or an organization. The bodies thus formed will have to conform to state and federal government laws and regulations governing such associations, especially if they are going to collect money from the public for their work. Modern civil rights movements may try to force both public and private organizations to be less exclusive than their founders intended. Names of organizations may be registered, so that no other group can take a name that is already being used.

It is implicit in this system that neither wealth nor wisdom, social position nor political power are necessary before a group of people may meet together, and form a committee or a more permanent organization. Nor is there any restriction on what any group of people may take as their purpose. A group of young mothers with only grade school educations may form a society to improve mental health in their town or to get the United Nations Declaration of Human Rights approved by the United States Congress or to promote universal peace. No one says, "You haven't the power, or the education, or the background, or the right to do this." Any movement, any new idea can take root anywhere, and any old idea may be backed by a new group of people.

People who start an organization and agree to abide by its rules form it along the lines of the Mayflower Compact. The members choose each other. Each person who joins, joins freely. No membership is irrevocable. Life memberships and honorary memberships are given: the former to those who wish to pay a fixed sum in lieu of annual dues, thus making a lifetime commitment to the work of the organization; the latter to individuals whom the group wishes to honor. And these memberships, also, may be resigned, or, if the individual member fails to live up to the purposes of the organization, may be revoked. Membership is thus seen as a choice made freely on both sides.

Citizenship by naturalization is a special kind of membership and follows, more or less, this pattern. It is given to an immigrant by the United States, can be freely resigned by the immigrant, and can be revoked by the United States government under certain circumstances. For example, an individual loses the right to be an American citizen if he makes false representations of any kind on his petition for citizenship, or if, prior to naturalization, he fails to obey the laws of the United States, which specifically include legislation defining acts that are incompatible with citizenship. However astounding it may be to Americans that those who have come here of free choice or who have been born here should wish to resign, nevertheless resignation is within the spirit of the American idea of a free pact that is freely entered into.

It is also the essence of American organization that commitments are well-defined and limited. The purpose of each organization is set forth, and no individual is expected to accept responsibility if the officers, the executive committee, or the board of directors go beyond the mandate given to them freely by the members. It is recognized that, as organizations grow larger, it is impossible for all the decisions to be made by the group as a whole. It is more efficient and wiser to have an executive committee or board conduct much of the routine business than to have a small, public meeting act as if if were, in fact, fully competent to make all the decisions. As the affairs of the organization get even larger, professional staff will be brought in; many board members, serving in a voluntary capacity and attending a few meetings a year, may lose touch with the details of what is going on.

Each of these steps, inevitable as an organization gets bigger and richer and takes on a greater variety of activities, causes friction. The smallest chapter of a national organization may follow the pattern of electing a board, but even as it does this, the members worry about turning over the conduct of an association to a smaller group that can, and must, act on its own. Even though board members are usually chosen from among the members, will serve for a limited term, and are to be returned, after serving, to ordinary membership, a sense of distance may grow up between them and the other members. With this may come some anxiety and distrust. Conflict between board or executive committee and the membership may even occur in groups that are very small.

There is a parallel in the relationships that exist between communities and state legislatures, and between states and the federal government. Conflict inevitably arises when tension between two parts of a total structure is treated as if it were a struggle between two rival groups, like the barons against the king in the days of the signing of the Magna Carta, the Commons against the king in the days of Cromwell, the American colonies against the British Crown, the states against the first, weak American Confederation, the House of Representatives against the United States Senate, the Congress as a whole against the executive branch of the government, or like smaller or weaker or less powerful groups in competition with each other. Essentially unwilling to give ultimate authority to any person or group of persons, yet recognizing the necessity of delegating authority, Americans, even as they delegate it, start restlessly watching that the legal, stated, written limits of the authority are not exceeded.

These attitudes are exceedingly important when it comes to forming, working in, and joining organizations. Each member is responsible only for what he understands the purpose of an organization to be, and for the open actions, openly reported, of the officers. The danger that these officers may exceed their power, and that the individual member may become responsible for something to which he did not give his full assent, is ever-present. And so voluntary organizations, free groups of people joined together to carry out self-selected and stated purposes, may incorporate under the laws of a state and receive the same protection that the stockholders and members of a board of directors of a business receive. The individual member is relieved from being personally responsible for all of the activities of the organization. If an organization is involved in legal proceedings, an officer cannot be held accountable until there is proof, not only that he was an official of a group that is criminally or civilly liable, but that he himself committed illegal acts with full knowledge of what he was doing. Incorporation has other advantages, too: it regularizes the ownership of property, it is easier to manage employment, and it gives the employees greater protection.

Good works performed by corporate bodies—

churches, schools, orphanages, and associations devoted to educational, patriotic, religious, or community welfare causes—entitle these bodies to tax-exempt status. These organizations pay no taxes on the land or buildings or stocks and bonds that they own, and individuals who make gifts to them are entitled to claim tax exemption for these contributions on their income tax returns, within certain specified limits.

The willingness of the body politic to let its citizens choose what they will support in the community, and to what extent, is the basis of the generosity of Americans, on the one hand, and their apparent stinginess with government funds on the other. When a man voluntarily decides that he will give away 30 percent of his income (perhaps 10 percent to his college that is in dire financial straits, 10 percent to a group working with retarded children, 5 percent to the Young Women's Christian Association for work with underprivileged young women, and 5 percent to the local hospital), he feels that he is really participating in these activities. The money he gives does, in a sense, represent him. This is the same feeling that is found in attitudes toward local government. Holders of property in a community feel that they are the people who should decide what is to be done there: whether the public money is to go for roads or schools, for a new sports stadium or a new library; whether the local tax rate is to be raised or lowered. The payment of the costs of any operation should, in this view, entitle one to have a voice in controlling it. All participation should be free, and freely entered into; those who join an organization should support it, and those who support it should control what is done with their support.

Most organizations in the United States have dues —the sum each member pays towards the cost of supporting his group. The dues may be very small, but they are a way of recognizing that only members whose dues are paid have a right to vote; and voting carries with it responsibility. It is the responsibility of the membership to be closely enough in touch with the way in which the elected officers and the employed staff are carrying out their delegated powers to be sure that everything is going all right.

One of the complications of government spending, above the community level, is that the people who contribute the funds through income taxes, excise taxes, sales taxes, and so forth, do not have any more control over how the money is spent than those who pay virtually no taxes at all. The poll tax as a voting requirement was, in effect, a payment of dues to the government. It was strictly in accord with the American sense of the relationship between contribution and control. But the poll tax offended another set of values, those embodied in the Fifteenth Amendment to the Constitution of the United States, and so was finally abolished. This means, from the standpoint of the taxpayer, that the principle of one man–one vote has been extended to include every adult, no matter whether he or she has paid any taxes or is actually entirely supported by the taxes of others, as in the case of minors and indigent adults. The control of state and federal government expenditures rests with voters, not taxpayers, and so the man who is a taxpayer is restive, in proportion to the size of his taxes, over the way in which government funds are spent. As a voter, he has only one vote; as a taxpayer, he may have made enormous contributions.

Another aspect of the American attitude toward giving is represented in the idea of a foundation, and foundations, in turn, play an important role in American life. A foundation is a trust fund established upon the death, or sometimes before the death, of a rich person who feels that some of his money should be returned to society and set aside for the poor or for his church or for educational purposes. This establishment of trusts, in which the purposes are carefully defined and legally specified, is very old, going back to the Middle Eastern practice of establishing trusts for religious institutions. In some old English bequests one finds the most minute specifications. For example: the size of pieces of meat to be distributed to the poor of a given city, once a year, on a given religious holiday. American bequests follow this trust fund pattern, and there are a great variety of funds, the proceeds of which are to go for the support of indigent white orphans, for example, or for scholarships to American Indians, or for college funds for girls descended from one of the first founders of the original Dutch colony in New York State (then called New Netherlands), and so on.

Such bequests were based, historically, on the idea that good works are an appropriate way for a rich man to return what he has made to God and to God's people. But trusts may be secular, and the idea of doing good may have become dissociated from the service of God, as making large donations has become dissociated from the idea of advancing the donor's own chances of getting into heaven. In any event, in the traditional trust the founders determined how the money was to be spent, and the executors merely carried out his will. If it became impossible to do so, the matter was settled by the courts. The perpetuation of the preferences and the prejudices of the dead, through the extension of his will, has been called the "dead hand," and institutions have often had to struggle to free themselves from the restrictions that dead benefactors have attempted to impose upon them.

Fortunately, some people state their purposes quite broadly when they set up trust funds. The money can then be spent, as time goes on, for dynamic programs that keep pace with advancing knowledge in the fields of special interest to the founders. The oldest foundation in the United States, The White-Williams Foundation of Philadelphia, Pennsylvania, is an organization of this kind. It was founded in 1800 by a group of seventeen men who wanted to "devise some plan of relief" for unwed mothers. It was first called The Magdalen Society, and the first "relief" was an "asylum" for unmarried girls expecting babies. The girls themselves rebelled against the institutional care provided, and when a special hospital was built for them, they rejected that, too.

In the early 1900's, after a long struggle between the board and the members, and within the board—on which women as well as men were by this time sitting—the society completely changed its approach to the problem of illegitimacy, and began to work through and with the Philadelphia Board of Public Education on a long-range program of prevention. This program eventually included a staff of trained social workers maintained in selected public elementary schools by the foundation to work with maladjusted children and their families, the first visiting teacher program of this kind in the United States; scholarships to enable bright but needy children to stay in school; an experimental Junior Employment Service in the Department of Compulsory Education of the Philadelphia public schools; and in-service training in social service methods for teachers and school principals.

Today, the White-Williams Foundation is still an independent, private organization, although its office is in the administration building of the Philadelphia Board of Public Education. It confines its work now to the scholarship program, helping about two hundred children a year on an annual scholarship budget of about $35,000. This program is limited only by the financial resources of the foundation, which receives no money from any public or private community fund. The work of the foundation is supported entirely by endowments and contributions from other trusts, individuals, and business firms.

The public has an interest in foundations because tax exemption, a privilege accorded to most of them by the government, is, in fact, a subsidy, and because very rich foundations may become too powerful. There are many local and state variations, but in many parts of the country American foundations are forbidden to engage in any political activities, and their actual expenditures are subject to review by the tax-collecting authorities and by Congress. There have been, however, no safeguards against the use of foundations by agencies of the federal government. The whole country was shocked by the revelation in early 1967 that the Central Intelligence Agency had been channeling funds through foundations. Although the purposes of these subsidies were often admirable, they were secret, and this procedure was felt to be inadmissible.

Many of the advances in medicine, education, science, and philanthropy that are benefiting people all over the world today have been possible only because American foundations have made gifts for the support of research and demonstration projects in the United States and many other countries, as well as grants administered by voluntary groups of responsible, public-spirited men and women, with the aid of imaginative professional staffs.

American foundations are often misunderstood abroad. Recipients of grants are inclined to believe that these organizations must have purposes other than those announced. Often, when foundations state as their purpose agricultural research or the promotion of international education, applicants assume hidden motives and try to learn what these are, assuming that if they meet these undeclared expectations they will be in line for more money. When they fail to find hidden purposes (for these do not usually exist) recipients are sometimes more convinced than ever of ulterior motives on the part of the foundation. But the foundation that works within the intent of the legal, economic, and ethical systems that make its existence possible is not allowed to have purposes beyond dispensing its money responsibly, within a program approved by the legally constituted board of directors and in accordance with the original purpose for which it was set up. Sometimes great foundations may set up smaller foundations, giving them more specific mandates, and thus safeguarding their own position, completely above the battle of immediate political aims.

This policy of being above the battle comes into collision with the hopes and aims of many Americans who are either for or against some cause which has wide ethical implications. If, for example, a foundation has been created for the announced purpose of promoting the educational status of Negroes, then it is open to no criticism if it promotes only education for Negroes; but if it was set up for general educational purposes and begins to specialize in work on Negro education alone, it will be subject to attacks from those who are opposed to any special treatment for Negroes. If it lets this criticism reduce its efforts, it will then be bitterly assailed by the proponents of such a policy. The belief in the correctness of political neutrality for churches, for foundations, indeed for most philanthropic organizations, seldom stands up completely when deeply held convictions become involved.

Furthermore, the practice of setting up tax-exempt funds for specific purposes has been extended. Institutions have been established that are exempt from taxation and yet able to exercise influence in directions congenial to the donors, who may be living men with great fortunes, or business corporations, or powerful industrial groups wishing to pursue certain kinds of research or promote specific educational aims. Groups of competing industries set up institutes that are supposed to be supported equally by all members, who will cooperatively contribute to research from which society, as well as the particular industries themselves, will benefit. Here again is an area where the general public interest, as in improved nutrition, and the specific private interests of a group of producers of special foods, like milk or meat, may become involved. At the community level, however, curricula for use in schools are often identified with a particular processor or manufacturer. Under such circumstances, the claim of disinterest of the foundations established by industry is hard to maintain and is continually suspect.

So the problem of maintaining disinterested concern for publicly stated purposes is always present for all American organizations. If any organization has a purpose greater than its dues-paying capacity, if wealthy donors—individuals, foundations, industries, or the government—participate, it is inevitable that the donors' wishes, expressed or simply perceived or misperceived by the recipients, will affect the policies of the organization. Professional organizations, however, may try to safeguard themselves against the influence of outside benefactors by limiting the voting power to active members, who pay smaller dues than associate members, although the latter often make substantial contributions.

Clearly, all of these considerations enter into the form that an organization takes. As its members must be responsible, because they have joined, it cannot have secret purposes. In spite of the fact that they have flourished on American soil, secret organizations obviously can be held to be against the public interest because their acts cannot be scrutinized. Members may not know the purposes until after they have joined. Equally, birthright membership is opposed to the American style; children who are made members at birth of an organization help to perpetuate a kind of nonvoluntary group that tends toward exclusiveness. Here, obviously, religious claims that the children of parents who follow a certain faith are born into it come into conflict with the general American position that each individual's religion, like his country, his occupation, his marriage, his political party, his political beliefs, are matters of free personal choice.

In the question of organizational responsibility, these issues of free choice, full consent, and full knowledge, have been heightened by the political events of the last thirty years. Those who preferred to think of being Jewish as a matter of choice, at a time when a man born to Jewish parents could elect what religion and what cultural stance he would take in the world, were shaken by Adolf Hitler's determined extermination of millions of people, merely because they were Jews or the descendants of Jews. The Communist Party assumption that membership in an organization, although itself an act of free will, is irrevocable—that one who has once joined the party is forever subject to its discipline without appeal—has influenced American attitudes toward responsibility.

For example, during the period rather immediately after World War II, it became customary for ex-Communists to denounce individuals as members of subversive organizations, simply because they had been present at meetings; and many legislators, feeling themselves to be inexperienced in the ways of foreign conspirators, were inclined to believe them. Guilt by association, an idea thoroughly repugnant to Americans, was dragged into quasi-political trials, and individuals were attacked because they had belonged to organizations which ex-Communists claimed had been infiltrated.

A clash is inevitable between the methods of political penetration Communism considers ethical and those considered ethical in a democracy. Here the question of secrecy is crucial. Secret organizations of any sort tend, in the American mind, to become conspiracies, either by members of an organization conspiring against the uninitiated public, or by officials of an organization involving the membership without their knowledge. As long as membership in an organization is a matter of free and open choice, and the purposes of the organization are openly declared and known to all the members, and as long as the acts of officers are reviewed and ratified by the whole membership, people feel that such an organization has a right to exist.

But, as in the conflict between local community responsibility and state and federal government action, the right to organize a group that freely chooses who may and who may not belong, and the right to choose narrow or chauvinistic aims, are challenged by the other American principle—the right of all men to equal opportunity for life, liberty, and the pursuit of happiness. The original Mayflower Compact was really extraordinarily narrow, a contract made freely with each other by a small group of men of the same race, from the same country, with the same dissident religious beliefs. Children, women, slaves, freedmen, the mentally ill, convicts, imbeciles, were all excluded from the full sense of this compact. They were beneficiaries only. Some of the male children would some day be full members, but the rest of the children would remain as wards of society for life.

Later, inspired by that model, the Constitution again envisaged a world of free contractual relationships between upstanding, tax-paying, property-owning, free, Christian, predominantly Protestant, white men. The history of the United States, especially the history of the broadening of the provisions of the Constitution and the growth of federal power, has been shot through with the effort to broaden, not the strength and beauty of the pact itself, but the definition of "all men," so that it should include women, members of other races, and all religions. The very fact that the members of other races came here under different auspices, which originally excluded them from the pact, has now become an argument for their inclusion. And the position of the American Indians—the original settlers who also had no rights under the pact but were treated essentially as foreigners unfortunately living on "our" territory, within which part of their former territory was now to be reserved for them—is even more anomalous.

The beginnings of the American idea of a free association of free men, acting in voluntary and consenting relationships to one another, with full responsibility for their own acts and with only such government as they themselves chose, although a great advance in its day, had to be subjected to a whole series of revisions. Two issues, full citizenship regardless of race and regardless of sex, have been fought out together, but in both cases, the preferences and prejudices and local situations in states and communities are still widely variant.

The passage of the Fifteenth and Nineteenth Amendments, in 1870 and 1920 respectively, guaranteed equal voting rights to all Americans, but the struggle for equality of opportunity is still going on in other directions. The Civil Rights Act of 1964 prohibits discrimination on the basis of race, color, religion, sex, or national origin by employers, labor unions, and employment agencies, and there will be a much fairer distribution of work opportunities for both men and women when this act reaches the point of complete enforcement in 1968. The Articles of the Constitution that guarantee equal rights for Negroes have been indifferently implemented at the local level in many states and properly implemented at social and economic levels in no part of the United States. The battle to secure these rights reached a climax when the Civil Rights Act of 1964 became the law of the land.

Conversely, the battle for the legal rights of adolescents has hardly begun. Our laws about what adolescents can and cannot do are so contradictory and discrepant that they violate almost every principle that Americans as a people have cherished: We believe there should be no taxation without representation, yet minors must pay taxes on their earnings even though they cannot vote. The right to bear arms and the obligation to answer the call to arms—the duty of every citizen—is also imposed on young American men who cannot vote. From the age of 16 to the age of 21—the legal age for voting and in almost all states, for drinking—minors are treated in a thousand contradictory and humiliating ways. The present increase in youthful violence, vandalism, and rioting has to be partly understood in the same terms as other demonstrations by those who do not feel that they have a voice in decisions about matters that concern them deeply.

This is especially true of college demonstrations.

American students have historically been less vocal than students in many parts of the world on political issues. Like students in English universities, they have been treated as politically voiceless, dependent minors, to be chaperoned, sent to bed, counted at night. For the most part, they have taken their restlessness out in childish pranks, pranks that would be held unworthy of politically minded and responsible young adults. As long as colleges were private institutions, run with private endowments, it could be argued that each college could set what conditions it wished. If a student did not want to conform, he could leave or be expelled. But as the public became increasingly involved in higher education at federal, state, and local levels, the right to expel, and even the right to exclude in the first place, became more and more dubious.

Once the right to vote and to determine policy was separated from the amount and kind of contribution the voter made, and once voting was established as the right of every citizen, regardless of color, creed, sect, or economic solvency and the budget of the community, state, or nation came to depend on votes, then the position of educational institutions changed. Students of both sexes on tax-supported campuses are now free to challenge the authorities, as women and members of other races have challenged public authority in the past.

Furthermore, the student today is often a husband, a father, a wage earner, and a taxpayer while still in school and before he is a voter. Although the civil rights movement for fuller participation and opportunity for Americans of African or Asian ancestry is better publicized today, the issues of the age at which a boy becomes a man and a girl becomes a woman—and the extent of their obligation to political commitments as long as they are without representation—is also being fought out, and is bound to be important in the future. Just as new countries have begun their constitutional lives by including votes for women and setting up safeguards against racial discrimination, the new question of what constitutes immaturity and maturity is also echoing around the world, expressing itself in student unrest.

Significantly, this is more a college question than it is a local community question. The young people of America are not rebelling against their parents or against their middle-aged neighbors or against the town fathers; they are rebelling against their status as half citizens–half children, and this rebellion is dramatized most vividly on college campuses, in state and national elections, and in the matter of conscription.

Again the pattern spreads. As women and children formed clubs and learned the rules, recited the great political truths on which the country was nourished, they too demanded the rights accorded so generously to "all men," and the definition of "all men" could no longer mean only white adult males. But it was white adult males, breaking with the traditional authority within their own society, rebelling against institutions of tyranny, authority, intolerance, and exploitation, who did, in fact, lay the groundwork on which other groups could claim their rights, also.

So the right to organize, today, is circumscribed by the conditions under which an organization is tax-exempt, and by the efforts to force all sorts of institutions to include members of minority groups. Organizations are slowly becoming less free to establish the terms of membership. The right to choose one's associates, even in the worship of God or in the pursuit of good works, is being balanced by the claim that full membership in the wider American society should not be denied to any American-born or naturalized citizen.

As the membership of organizations becomes thus formalized and organizations are put under pressure to widen their membership, individual responsibility declines, and the sense of individual initiative is also somewhat endangered. A trade union to which one must belong, because of a government-supervised election, has a very different call upon one's loyalties than a trade union for whose existence one fights, against both management and government. A school to which one's own child and all other children must go does not involve parents as deeply as a school they havè chosen for their children. A college fraternity that is forced by democratic opinion to select new members among nominees, by lot, hardly has the same cohesion as the group that is free to make and promote its own invitations. High school clubs that are part of the school curriculum have less appeal than the clubs that the students form themselves because they want to practice their French or Russian, or because they want to talk about social and political affairs. The club or church that one must join because it is *the* club or *the* church that is suitable for the family of a rising junior executive in a given large company hardly represents either a free social or free religious choice.

It is in the face of such dilemmas and the outside pressures that are developing with America's soaring population, and the increasing involvement in everyday life of state and federal government, that organizations have to discover how to keep the sense of choice, commitment, involvement, and excitement going. The strength of community initiative lies in the right of association, the right of choice, and the responsibility to choose to do something about those things that need doing. A prayer written by the celebrated theologian Reinhold Niebuhr and used by many organizations expresses this attitude:

> Oh God:
> Give me the serenity to accept
> what cannot be changed,
> Give me the courage to change
> what must be changed,
> The wisdom to distinguish one
> from the other.[2]

---

[2] This prayer is quoted here by permission of the author. It was distributed by the Federal Council of Churches among the soldiers of World War II, and was subsequently adopted in somewhat altered form by Alcoholics Anonymous.

VIII Struggles Within Organizations

When there is a new task to be carried out, people in every country turn first to their traditional ways of getting things done. One of the favorite themes of fiction is that of a group of strangers stranded on a desert island who have to work out new patterns of organization for their lives by drawing on past experience. Old ideas of how things are done crowd into people's minds in emergencies, and the same forms, slightly altered to meet the new circumstances, recur and recur.

In early Christianity, new ideas were embodied in religious orders. When a Christian had an inspiration that gave him new insight into the meaning of life, he would seek permission to found a new order based on his theory, as when St. Dominic perceived that work could be a form of prayer and started the Dominican order, devoted to work and prayer. Later, St. Ignatius, primarily interested in the spread of the teachings of Jesus Christ, founded the Jesuits to carry out his special conception of Christianity. Today there are "third" orders of laymen who accept special religious rules of life. Within this cultural pattern, it is the idea that counts, and founders seek out other like-minded persons to join with them, live with them, and carry out the new principles. This European religious style still prevailed when the early Protestant sects—like-minded men and women seeking to form a new kind of community life—began to develop.

But there was one essential difference between the Christian communities of the Roman Catholic and Eastern Orthodox Churches and the communities of Protestantism: the Roman Catholic and Eastern Orthodox orders consisted of individuals of the same sex, who did not marry, while the Protestant communities were formed from families. Groups of men, women, and children, seeking the same way of life, formed themselves into communities; more children were born to them, and where the first generation had been nonconformist, even revolutionary in its ideas, the next generation was brought up rigidly in the ideas of the founding group. Initially, newcomers were eagerly welcomed because they built up the strength of the tiny communities that set off by sea and by land to brave the dangers of travel in order to escape from the persecution of governments who considered their way of life subversive.

But in the next generation these communities often closed themselves in; recruits now came from their children and their children's children. They ceased to look for new members, and the various devices they had adopted as signs of their way of life, such as special "plain dress," grey or black or brown, often the dress of very simple people, to show their humility, became a sign of belonging to a chosen group. Where they had once been poor, they often became very prosperous, as they were people who allowed themselves few pleasures or indulgences and who worked hard together for the glory of God.

A religious order of celibate members can recruit, generation after generation, like-minded people who will enter it for life and be strictly trained to follow the rules.

Those who find the requirements too difficult will be weeded out. Recruitment will be helped by teaching: many religious orders teach, in one way or another; nursing orders run hospitals and take young girls to train as nurses; teaching orders teach in schools, where bright young people may be identified and inducted. Sometimes the religious emphasis is so strong in a society that every child will have some experience of what the religious life is like, as when all young men in traditional Burma spent a few months within a Buddhist monastery to which they could always return. In Ireland the celibate religious life was so revered that every family hoped to dedicate one member to the exclusive service of the church, and even those who did not enter the church often put off marriage to a late date or did not marry at all.

When members of a religious group become missionaries in a foreign country, the need to win converts may be so great that there is very little room to train children for secular tasks, especially if the mission is expanding. So where in an old established country an order of celibate clergy is a way of emphasizing one particular life choice, in an expanding situation a church may try to recruit almost all of the children and absorb their lives, very much as the noncelibate communities do. As long as the rule is celibacy, the community must always be reaching out for new members. When the spirit that guided the founding of the order or the particular monastery fails or changes, then those orders die out, as is happening today in the famous old monasteries of the Orthodox world.

There is, therefore, a strong contrast between the community that is celibate and must always recruit new members, and the community that, once started, can reproduce itself. Although those within it are cloistered and governed by strict rules, the celibate order faces out. The community of men, women, and children faces in, and after a while, newcomers are not wanted. It may even be necessary to find new places for the next generation, in which case groups will leave the parent body and form exact imitations of the parent community somewhere else.

Each such community feels it has the perfect way of life, down to the number of buttons on a man's coat, the rules about how men and women should address each other, where they should sit, and how they should sit. Only by absolute obedience and conformity to the established rules can such a community survive at all. To doubt the importance of the smallest detail is to question the whole structure. Those religious communities that formed an important part of early American settlements were of the uncompromising type—Pilgrims from England, Puritans from England, Covenanters from Scotland, Huguenots from France, Quakers from England, Moravians from Bohemia, Mennonites from Germany. Controversies developed over small differences, and a part of the group, challenging the older members, would set off to found its own community. As these originally rebellious splinter groups brought up their children, they, in turn, would demand absolute conformity.

Not only Christian religious groups, but Jewish groups, also, showed this pattern. The small Jewish communities struggled to hold the next generation by insisting upon a way of life requiring continual vigilance. The members of an Orthodox Jewish community dressed in a prescribed fashion, ate meat slaughtered in a special way, kept special rules for the Sabbath, and fasted on special days. Their way of life, like the way of life of the "plain people" of the various Protestant Christian sects, kept them together. Every effort was made to keep young people from leaving the group, and outsiders, even converts, were greeted unenthusiastically.

A third form of association was based on a common occupation rather than a common religious belief and had its prototype in the old European guilds, in which a master craftsman took apprentices into his house. The apprentices lived with him, giving him the kind of allegiance a child owes a parent. He, in turn, cared for the apprentices with the obligation of the parent toward his children. Here again the emphasis was the passing on of a tradition. People trained the children of other members of the craft. But there was always a double fear: that there would be too many craftsmen and not enough work for each, and that the craft skills and secrets would be lost because too few of the children of craftsmen would want to be craftsmen themselves.

This type of organization, emphasizing both descent and narrow membership, is still found in the American craft unions, among printers, for example, where the right to obtain training and join the union is passed on from father to son. In such closed groups, where people think of the number of positions as limited but hope that their children can obtain them, another exclusive tendency grows up: the men born into such a group tend to marry women born into the group.

The more narrowly specialized the life associated with a man's occupation, as, for example, with the career of a naval officer, a civil aeronautics pilot, or a nuclear physicist, the greater the demand for women who will understand the special requirements of the way of life; and where can they be found except among the daughters of other members of the group? So, also, where farming is practiced by only a part of a population, farmers realize they must marry farmers' daughters; city girls will never have the skills, the endurance, and the patience needed on the farms. And fishermen must find their wives among other fishermen's daughters; miners, among miners' daughters, women who will understand and tolerate the special kinds of dangers their men undergo.

In medieval Europe, there were some even more tightly closed groups, a few of which came to America. The Gypsies were one of these. They jealously kept themselves apart from the people among whom they lived, spoke their own language, and dressed their women in ways so conspicuously different that they were protected from the advances of non-Gypsy men.

When American Indian groups were no longer the proud possessors of great hunting grounds, they still attempted to keep their tribal identity by wearing distinctive dress, especially requiring this for their women, still speaking their own language, and accustoming their children to a way of life that was different from the ways of the wider world.

If we look at these various forms of association— men and women and, later, children originally grouped freely around an idea—it is easy to see that the principle of narrowness, of exclusiveness comes in whenever the idea of special vocation is added to the idea of descent. This is either real descent, so that children of both sexes live the way their parents have lived, or pseudodescent, as children, pupils, or apprentices are absorbed into the lives of their teachers and masters.

When the work one does, the religious and political ideas of the good life, the choice of a wife, the rearing of the children, and the place where one lives are all bound together, then the tendency to exclusiveness is very great indeed. If, additionally, such groups live and work together in the same places, base their way of life on a common place of residence—as when craftsmen live in their shops; or the army and navy, even within their own countries, have special compounds; or when big companies build special suburbs for their executives— the emphasis comes to be put on the perpetuation of the group, both of its ideas and of its membership. Newcomers are admitted only after undergoing harsh or prolonged and expensive initiation, and, on the whole, are welcomed only when such a group cannot perpetuate itself by breeding enough children.

In any society, the tendency toward forming groups of this kind is always present, and when people of different religions and different ethnic backgrounds live in close association, it becomes even greater. The Middle

East is an outstanding example of a region where the association between religion, style of life, and occupation—even to one religious group being goldsmiths and another silversmiths—was highly developed. When the emphasis is carried to an extreme degree, one finds caste systems, such as those of traditional India, where work and marriage choice are tightly associated, and the production of another generation that will go on doing what its fathers did is the principal form of recruitment.

The United States inherited all of these possibilities. A great number of the early settlements were closed religious communities; others tended toward adopting tightly patterned ways of life, forcing out those who did not agree with them. In a crowded and ancient country such as India, many groups come to terms with each other because they live in such close quarters that the fear of too close contact is as strong as the need for the services rendered by another caste. But in the United States, where there has been so much room, it has always been possible for the dissenters or the people with new ideas to leave a group, individually or with their followers. All sorts of promised lands lay just in the next valley or over the next hill. The way to live one's own life was to move somewhere else and set up another tight, rigid, little group.

Only in the southeastern part of the United States did people try to substitute social distance for physical distance. In the early days, the slaves lived on the plantations, close to the masters, who had to care for them when they were ill and generally take responsibility for them, while they, in turn, reared the master's children. Here social distance—rules about eating together, terms of address, which door people entered, separation on certain occasions when traveling and in school—took the place of geographical distance. Today, the people of the rest of the country deal with all sorts of strangers and foreigners by simply not associating with them. They do this primarily by housing devices that will make sure that the children of minority groups will go to different schools and play on different playgrounds. They are puzzled by Southerners who happily turn their children over to Negro nurses and are deeply shocked by southern rules discriminating between whites and Negroes while keeping them close together. Each group sees the traditional race relations of the other as harsh and repellant, complicating the task of changing attitudes toward race differences on a national scale.

In the United States, there is a continuous battle between the tendency to form exclusive social groups, to which one's children of both sexes will belong and from which other people can be kept out, and the demand that every member of the total society shall have freedom of movement and the right to any social or economic privilege possessed by anyone else. People are always forming new clubs and societies dedicated to some purpose, established to do something, set up to enjoy something, or to fix something. Then, in time, the club or society becomes associated with certain kinds of privilege. A nature club may be founded by a woman who likes taking children on bird walks; later, adults join it, and slowly it assumes a quality of exclusiveness and gets the reputation of being hard to get into. Then individuals may want to join, not because they care about birds, but because it will be a step upward socially to belong.

Sometimes organizations start as purely local. Other towns hear about them and form similar groups of their own. After several of these have been started, someone proposes that they get together to have a conference or convention to discuss their common interests. Out of such meetings, state organizations and later national organizations emerge, obtain charters, and regularize the ways in which new groups connected with the new national body can be founded. Sometimes the national organization will be conceived as one great whole, of which local organizations are branches, like the branches of a tree, and sometimes as a federation, in which each local group is thought of as a more or less independent unit which has chosen to join. In practice, the two patterns are very much alike. For example, a group of women who have graduated from college may found a college club whose main purpose is to raise money for scholarships to send local girls to the university. In time, some member may decide that this is too narrow a purpose, that the local college club should become a branch of the American Association of University Women, which, in turn, is a member of the International Federation of University Women. There will be arguments and discussions about this. Whether or not to become a branch of a national association is an important decision for a local group to make. It means a new set of obligations, new standards of membership. A certain percentage of the dues that local members pay must go to the national office. When these local women had their own little college club, they themselves could decide who could belong. Members did not even have to be college graduates; they could just have gone to a college, almost any kind of college, and still be eligible; for in the United States, higher education varies from small two-year colleges, where the teaching may be very poor, to colleges that are parts of great universities.

There are in general three ways in which organizations can get and keep members who do not otherwise have the correct qualifications. One of these is a device called a "grandfather clause," used especially by professional organizations (teachers, nurses, social workers) or associations of people seeking professional status for occupations which have not previously been recognized as professions (interpreters, insurance salesmen, real estate operators, public relations men, advertisers) which set new, higher requirements for admission of new members but will allow earlier members to stay.

Another device is a type of membership called "associate," for people interested in the same things as the members but ineligible for regular membership because they do not meet the requirements. Being "interested in the same things" often means that the interested person has given or is willing to give something to the organization, usually time or money. Sometimes it costs more to be an associate than it does to be an active member.

A third way of making people members of an organization, even when they are not very much interested but the organization wants the lustre of their names, is to elect them as honorary members. This privilege is sometimes extended to distinguished foreigners who would not be eligible if one of the requirements is for citizenship. A variation of this is the life membership— a way of recognizing a member who worked very hard at the beginning, or someone who has retired from business or profession and can no longer afford the dues, or someone who will pay a lifetime of dues in advance so that the organization will have funds to work with in the present.

With all of these devices, organizations go through stages of being very local, of becoming ambitious national organizations looking for new members, of worrying about whether standards will fall or whether some new element may get control of the organization, of making it harder for local branches to get recognition, of finding that it is short of money and therefore needs to establish some other form of membership, or of finding that it is not "reaching" some part of the population that should supply new members but is not doing so. Someone will start a program to interest students in membership upon graduation, and that action, in turn, may assume proportions that alarm some of the older members. It may take only a small issue which appeals to youth, members who do not yet really have much experience, to start action that is not quite in the spirit of the organization.

And there are further complications. Most voluntary organizations depend upon the members' doing all the work themselves. When they are small, they usually meet in someone's home, which is one reason they tend to be exclusive, as membership gets tied up with the question of whom you would ask to your house.

Thus it is that the very institutions that make it so possible to form organizations in the United States, such as the willingness to invite strangers into the very heart of one's own home, also set in motion all sorts of small snobberies. People try to get into organizations so as to get inside certain homes; homes will be "opened" for benefit performances because people want to get inside them, and, in turn, clubs may be narrow and exclusive because they want to go on meeting in "that lovely old house."

About twenty years ago, in a southern city, the white wife of the white president of a predominantly Negro institution was asked if she would continue her predecessor's custom of entertaining the local branch of the American Association of University Women. She did so, and for the first time Negro members of the faculty of the institution were invited. Here, hospitality, tradition, and a desire to continue to use the beautiful old colonial house as a meeting place were all brought into play to change the local, exclusive pattern of social life.

When an organization gets too big for a member's house, or at least for any but a fairly rich member's house, then a next step has to be taken: The group must find a meeting place. Here, again, the conflict between a more inclusive group and a more exclusive one may come up. As the organization gets bigger and less exclusive, it may cross lines that have not previously been crossed socially. There may be new members who come from religious, national, or racial groups that have been excluded from a country club or have never stayed at an exclusive hotel. New crises arise. Sometimes the organization boycotts a hotel that discriminates against some of the members; sometimes a club or hotel will lower the bars for an organization on a special occasion and then put them up again for the rest of the year.

Another kind of situation also occurs when an organization crosses ordinary social lines because its members are intent on some particular point, such as racial equality or recognition or nonrecognition of a foreign country. People of many different backgrounds may be members, and the club or hotel selected for a meeting by one part of the group may prove to be completely unfamiliar to other participants. One noisy, disorderly meeting, in which people accustomed to rough floors in smoky old halls drop their cigarette ashes all over the carpets, may ruin a hotel's reputation.

So the battles about who is to belong and what the social style is to be extend to the question of meeting places outside the home and to the problem of where national conventions can be held. When a group that has formerly been denied, or has not been interested in, this kind of social opportunity begins coming up in power and importance, the ability to hold social functions at big hotels is one of the first signs that they have joined the mainstream of American social life. Meanwhile, in small towns, one or two small hotels may proudly post a list of the clubs that meet there regularly for weekly lunches.

The hotel itself is one of the very special institutions of American life. Here, in spacious, sometimes atrociously, sometimes attractively, almost always flamboyantly decorated salons and corridors, and in suites of all sizes, people who have never stayed in a hotel in their lives may meet or dine or hold conventions and committee meetings. The daughter of a domestic worker may stay at the most exclusive hotel in town on her wedding night, provided she has no visible marks of belonging to a group that does not habitually use such hotels. She would be turned away if she arrived barefoot or looked as if she never wore shoes. And so we have the kind of rules that also get spread to American-owned hotels abroad: the rule, for instance, that every man who enters the dining room must wear a necktie, a rule that disregards the customary dress of other countries. The management of the hotel feels that at any moment the establishment may be overwhelmed by the wrong kind of guests, that its standards may fall, or that the right kind of traveler or guest may no longer arrive.

And these fears are almost always justified, because in such an exceedingly mixed society, with people bringing the manners of many different countries together, only the most simple external conformity can be depended upon. While there are ways of speaking and acting in the United States that definitely proclaim that people come from limited or provincial or cosmopolitan or working class or unacculturated foreign peasant backgrounds, there is no certainty at all as to what accent, manner, or style can reliably indicate a middle-class or upper-class position. Clubs and hotels can only insist on outward conformity in such matters as suitable clothing or where cigarette ashes are put.

And there is another point where the openness of the American home, and the parallel of the home with the hotel, matches American ideas about inclusiveness and exclusiveness: In a society where hundreds of thousands of children in one city may be natives while their parents remain foreign in manners, there is a tremendous discrepancy between the parents and the children's guests. Young people, asked to a schoolmate's home, seldom know what to expect. Parents in turn are in a continual state of nervousness about whom their children may bring home. Will they come from a higher social level, or a lower? When people are very poor, as during a depression, or when they live in an underprivileged neighborhood, the custom of bringing friends home may disappear altogether, and young people will meet each other somewhere else. But even when young people bring friends home easily, the parents are likely to be disregarded, or may stay in the background, either because they are afraid of the visitors or afraid of embarrassing their children.

So the possibility of having one's home invaded by a group of strange adolescents or by a group of women who belong to the same organization but whom one hardly knows is an ever-present one, unknown in societies where homes are tightly guarded against strangers and all meetings are held in cafes or public buildings. Yet the essence of American association is still a small group of people who know each other well enough to meet in each other's homes or in the homes of prominent men or women, persons whose names are well-known. The home meeting, however, must expand into a meeting called in some more formal place if strangers are to be given an open invitation.

The need for more and larger public meeting places is a crying one in most communities. The preferred meeting places are almost always schools and churches, and to an extent these symbolize two aspects of the community —a central concern for the children, and the tendency to establish groups of like-minded people. The public school or the public hall or the community room of a department store or the hotel dining room is a place where any group should be able to call a meeting. The church and the private club are places to which people have to be invited. American communities are forever getting these two confused, objecting to public meetings addressed by leaders who are regarded as radical or reactionary, and demanding that all private meeting places be open to anyone who wants to use them for meetings.

But there is the counterclaim, based on the idea of the old, like-minded religious community in which everyone who enters must conform completely, and all children who are reared there must, if they stay, remain rigidly conforming members of a group which itself began with a fine, rebellious, idealistic flame. And there is sometimes the feeling that every building in town should be regarded as an extension of the idea that every man's home is his castle, once the citizen's defense against the tyranny of kings and nobles. Then the townspeople can put up signs announcing that certain categories of persons are not wanted in the community after sunset, or they can establish a curfew and send all the children to bed at a certain hour, or put up a police line and turn back youngsters in cars coming from some other town.

On the other side are those who feel that there should be laws against exclusiveness in any meeting place, any club, any boardinghouse, and any playground. These people insist that, far from extending the home into the town (which can then be embattled against every other town), the state, and even the federal government, each home is only a home as long as only the family members use it.

There are endless small furors in the United States over some new aspect of this question of exclusiveness and inclusiveness, such as the refusal of some local group to bury an American Indian veteran in the veterans' cemetery, or the refusal of a country club to allow Negro friends of members to dine there. Feelings run high, both sides harden their lines, and readers abroad, who live in countries where burying grounds have been segregated for centuries along the most minute lines of sect, lineage, occupation, and residence, may be shocked to find that such a question is debatable in the United States, which is so often set up as a model of democracy. But in the United States each of these issues is considered separately. It may be an argument about who is to borrow books from the library or where people are to be buried. Or the question may be, should the Council of Social Agencies, which includes minority groups of various kinds, have its annual dinner at an exclusive country club where, for the rest of the year, admission is limited by class, color, religion, and ability to pay? Each issue is blown up to enormous proportions. Presidents resign from clubs that are suddenly found to be practicing discrimination, and this news appears abroad as an example of dreadful behavior on the part of a particular organization when it is actually an example of the continuous struggle of a heterogeneous and open society to keep the society open and yet permit groups to have enough coherence to be able to act as groups.

The formation of various kinds of secret and semi-secret societies is another form which the exclusiveness-inclusiveness issue takes. In American universities, particularly the big state universities open to all, Greek letter fraternities are an important way of sorting out the students. They give small groups of students places to live and are a means of maintaining contact between former graduates and the present college generation. They start as ways of organizing groups of students who have somewhat the same kinds of background and income. But then begins the whole question of whom to take in and whom to keep out. Local fraternities and sororities form federations; the federations establish standards and promulgate rules. The local group has to get enough members to support its living arrangements; it has to get the kind of members who, if they transfer to another university, will be acceptable to the members of another chapter of the same fraternity.

So the national fraternal organization presses for standards which would be less necessary if no one moved. But, as in all nationwide federations of organizations, members do move. Great differences in style between different parts of the country, different towns or university campuses, result in confusion. So the national organization attempts to standardize entrance requirements. But the national organization is also beset with pressures toward being more democratic and more inclusive. Again we find the anomaly of some nationwide fraternities trying to insist on greater breadth of membership, thus repudiating the very reason the fraternities were founded, and we find others backing up local chapters in their exclusiveness, risking mass resignations or secessions.

Meanwhile, high school students who do not expect to go to college form Greek letter fraternities so they can copy the exclusiveness they see as the major appeal of the college fraternities. Small groups of fraternity men on campuses where most of the students are day students intent on working their way through college, with no time for community activities, see themselves as especially responsible and embattled groups. Negro colleges, led by the advocates of an otherwise open society, approve the founding of exclusive, national, Negro fraternities that will divide their own campuses into those who are in and those who cannot get in. Labor leaders who have fulminated against special privilege hold their meetings at the most exclusive resort hotels or at union headquarters modeled after the board rooms of big executives. Jewish leaders who have protested against the exclusion of Jews from private country clubs help finance Jewish fraternities on college campuses.

A community-spirited organization may also be caught in the same dilemma. It will make a survey of the resources of its community, count its schools, libraries, hospitals, its service organizations, the number of high school graduates who go to college, and the amount of public money spent on each school child. Then, at a local meeting, after the survey has been finished and the members are justifiably proud of the fine town it has shown theirs to be, someone raises the question: Should we distribute this? If we do, won't a lot of undesirable people from the slums of the city move out here to get these advantages for their children, swamp our schools, and ruin just what we have worked so hard to build? Maybe we had better not distribute this booklet after all.

On the other hand, on the other side of this same city, a group that is developing a new center, to which it hopes to attract new industry, will collect all the surveys of the area that have been made and publish a big, glossy book with lists of all the nearby communities with fine schools, churches, little theaters, libraries, beaches, tennis courts, golf clubs, and swimming pools, for the very purpose of attracting people to these communities. Studies of American cities have shown that the town that is growing is also the town that is developing better services for everyone in it and will have the highest expenditures for social services, the best cultural institutions: concerts, an opera house, an orchestra, a small museum, and so forth. To improve, it must grow.

But the dilemma that faced the earliest colonists remains: To be a good town, you must have enough of the right kind of people. The right kind of people are responsible people, people with enough money, time, and education to be able to serve the community, give their time and effort to organizations, sit on boards, serve on committees, go as delegates to state or national conventions, argue with public officials at city, state, and national levels. A town is called a good town when it is a responsible town, with fine schools, adequate provisions for youth, enough hospital beds, all facilities primarily dependent upon local income from taxes and local private generosity. This means that a good town is a place which attracts people who want good services, more grass on which their children can play, better schools for their children, better hospitals in which their babies can be born, better chances for high school children to win scholarships.

But if too many people who need services crowd into a town, the services become overburdened, taxes go up, landowners are inclined to move away, even to sell, and there are fewer people to provide for and care for the people who came there originally because it was a place where their needs could be met. Meanwhile, groups who on other issues oppose each other struggle together to bring in even more people who need services: private industry, which needs more cheap labor or more skilled labor or more technical personnel; the Chamber of Commerce, which is committed to the industrial growth of the town; or generous, tolerant members of the community who believe that every community should open its arms to those in need, that is is wrong to refuse anyone, be they hopeless refugees from drought-stricken areas, in broken-down cars, non-English-speaking people, or rural people whose children, accustomed to the woods, vandalize everyone's front garden.

Against this kind of growth stand the old inhabitants, the wealthier, the more established—and the poor —none of whom wish to share what they have with people whom they consider beneath them because of creed or color, or because they have come more recently into the region or the country.

If the old inhabitants win, we call the community reactionary and point out also that it is "cutting off its nose to spite its face"; that a community afraid of labor unions may at first get a few industries beset by labor troubles to move there. But later on, if the community remains unfriendly to the stranger and is unwilling to deal with the outmoded barriers among the local inhabitants, it will find it difficult to attract industry.

This is in general how the growth and development of towns and cities proceeds, with periods when new people are welcomed and periods when they are feared. Sometimes it is the old English-speaking inhabitants who try to stop the influx of new people; sometimes it is the established members of a minority group who do not want their hard-won reputation for respectability and industry jeopardized by the arrival of another group of people of their own race or nationality, with country habits, who will not know how to live in a city.

In each part of the country, and often in two towns in the same state, there will be great differences. And sometimes the most expected differences are reversed. So to the people in a city in upstate New York, "race relations" did not mean relationships between the older white and the new Negro populations, but relationships between the English-speaking and the Polish people, many of whom were third generation. A small town in California may complain about its difficulties with a migrant population, meaning not its own minority group —Mexicans from just over the border—but "those poor white people from the dust bowl we don't know what to do with."

The prevailing themes, then, are: older inhabitants

distrustful of newcomers who may at the same time be needed and welcomed by part of the community, and the tendency, sometimes reversed, for the group that is most conspicuously descended from early English-speaking immigrants to consider itself intrinsically superior to anyone who shows visible signs of having other ancestry. But sometimes this superiority is only a demand for a change of one's name. For example, in some companies promotion to higher levels in plant and office may depend upon having "English-sounding" names.

People from every corner of the globe—some arriving wealthy, many more arriving poor, some with an education, many more without an education, some looking like the early settlers and some looking extraordinarily different—have tried and are trying to work out the problems involved in becoming one people, a people who can trust each other in peace and in wartime. The styles of American life reflect this process at every turn.

And the process is also reflected in the composition of organizations designed to better the town or help some group in the wider world. An organization will be formed by a small group of town leaders who associate their superior social position with social responsibility or with the management of the museum, the art gallery, or the library. Then there will come a period of broadening the base, an attempt to reach new people. The social bars that surrounded the members of the board will dissolve, as new money or new people are brought in, or the group will be broadened to include a wider range. So in the 1940's family welfare societies were formed of all the groups in the community working for the welfare of women and children. This meant that the formal religious invocation with which they opened their meetings had to be more inclusive, and the formula—"minister, priest, and rabbi"—that was spreading over the country in response to growing horror at Hitler's regime in Germany was adopted. At the same time, a group of responsible Negro leaders began appearing, often for the first time, at meetings which had once combined social responsibility with social snobbery.

Again there are striking reversals. In northern New England, the immigrants coming from French Canada during the nineteenth century were poor and unskilled. They were the least successful children of Canadian farm families; the farms and the education had gone to their more favored brothers. For many years, they were a voiceless and submerged section of the communities where they worked in the mills. The English-speaking American communities made no concessions; these immigrants, like all other immigrants before them, should learn English. The old inhabitants had dealt with all other immigrant groups who wished to remain in little enclaves and speak their own language by a very simple device: compulsory education which, in English-speaking schools, assured the children enough English to be able to function in American society. Even such well-intentioned attempts as the preparation in French of information about what foods to eat in wartime were resisted by the indigenous English-speaking population. But suddenly the people of one small New England city woke up to find the invitations to the mayor's reception written in *French*. The French Canadians, or Franco-Americans as they call themselves in the United States, had become numerous enough to take over town politics, and the old inhabitants found *their* mayor, in *their* city, speaking to them in a language which revived the memory of the French and Indian wars, when the conflict between England and France in Europe had involved English and French colonists and Indian allies in the New World.

The old attitudes of patronage and exclusiveness do not die; they are simply overpowered temporarily by some new wave of inclusiveness or some new practical need. The ideal of an inclusive, open society and the ideal of an exclusive like-mindedness both survive.

IX Public and Private Responsibilities

In the United States, a letter written on the stationery of an organized group gets a hearing. Here, one person who speaks in the name of an organization speaks with the strength of ten, if not 10,000. In Great Britain, a single question in Parliament sends a minister scurrying to provide an answer. But individuals who want to affect policy in the United States must organize to be heard, whether they are trout fishermen who want to keep the streams from being polluted or beauty lovers who want advertising billboards barred from the freeways or parents of blind children who want special schools for their children. The alternative is to act through an organization to which one already belongs, persuading its local, state, regional, or national office to take up one's cause.

Organizations are the way in which the individuality of Americans is expanded and optimized and through which any voice with a strong enough purpose behind it can be amplified. As individuals have many purposes, so do organizations, and in both cases, these purposes may conflict. For example, a woman may belong to a local branch of the American Association of University Women that is bringing pressure on local officials to build a public library, and to a taxpayers' association that is fighting the plan because it will mean higher taxes, and to a special committee that is trying to keep for a wildlife park the site that has been chosen for the library.

In the same way, a doctor may be a leader in a local mental health society that wants the community to have a psychiatric hospital, and a member of a county medical society that has taken a strong stand against the building of a specialized hospital and would rather add a wing for mental patients to the present general hospital. Or he may be an officer in an organization opposing the local use of federal government funds because of the rules against racial discrimination that go with grants of federal money. At the same time he may be the chairman of a committee investigating charges of religious prejudice in the administration of a local college. For him, all of these are partial goals; few people are equally active in two organizations with conflicting aims, such as a Parent-Teacher Association and a taxpayers' association, but they may pay dues to both. It is part of the complexity of American life that very seldom, even on the extreme right or the extreme left, are people consistent in the groups they join or the causes they espouse.

Because the country is so large and so diverse, and because regions and states and cities differ from each other so much, the national policies of any national organization may be quite different from the policies of many of its state and local branches. So people who have moved to a new community and expect to fit in there with the local branch or chapter of some organization with which they have been happily associated in some other part of the country may be grievously disappointed. Then too, organizations change their policies and sometimes their purposes. They come to have lives of their own; and as times change and causes alter—as a cure for a disease is found, or the public authorities take over a responsibility —new tasks are undertaken to occupy some of the same membership and use the accumulated funds.

One important general principle about voluntary organizations in the United States is that they can do certain things that public agencies cannot do, such as advocate partisan courses of action, experiment with new ideas which may fail, and act with greater freedom from rules and regulations. Most public agencies at the local, state, or federal level have civil service requirements for professional people. This means that a social worker or an educator or a physician who works in public service has to meet formal requirements with respect to education, age, previous experience, and so forth, and must keep his activities within the limits officially determined for his agency. There will be rules about office hours; rules stating the times when political activity is permitted and when it is not; rules about the times when a staff member may take the initiative and when he must wait for someone else to move first. While such rules are necessary and seem almost inevitable in a society where people think of public officials as their servants, they do limit the amount of freedom most government employees have in connection with their work.

It has been a long, uphill road to separate professional work in government from the political spoils system, in which the supporters of successful political candidates get jobs as rewards. There has also been a similar struggle against the practice of nepotism, and the government has had to make rules about that, too. Many new countries are facing these same problems, and one of the causes of friction in programs in which old and new countries work together is that the old countries once had a system of political favoritism, which they have to a large extent learned how to eliminate, and so they are very impatient with new countries when they feel that too many tasks which require professional training and skill are given to relatives of powerful political figures.

This was once true in the United States. One nationality group, or even the immigrants from one part of a country, such as Ireland, would get control of some public service maintained by taxes. Cousin after cousin would arrive, totally unused to the ways of the new country, and be put into a well-paying job on the police force, in the fire department, or at the zoo. As a result, there are a great many rules today to prevent this, some even prohibiting husband and wife from working at the same time in the same publicly financed university.

Perhaps new countries will be able to deal with this problem better than we have. Perhaps they will find ways to make some of their great families responsible for preparing their members to contribute the ideas and initiative their country needs. This would be highly beneficial, for it would mean that high standards and family ties would go together instead of working against each other. This, in a sense, is what happened in the family of the late President Kennedy. Members had been educated to such a high level of skill, in anticipation of public service, that the family could provide prime government leadership when it was needed. Such leadership is valuable and is in direct contrast to the shabby use of personal influence to add relatives—brothers, cousins, nephews, sons, wives, and daughters—to the payrolls of government offices.

And tax-supported institutions often have other handicaps. In some parts of the country, there are rules that insist on no discrimination by race or religion in public service. This may mean that the public service will be crowded by members of a minority group because it is the only place they can get employment; and, in turn, majority group members may tend to go into other fields. It may mean that the best people who apply for public jobs, although they are the best of those who apply, may not be very well trained because they go into public service for other reasons than simply professional ones. Often the more enterprising and imaginative people will prefer the greater freedom of a private agency, sometimes even at lower salaries.

Veterans receive preference in most public agencies, and this again may mean discrimination against a more qualified person, especially in the case of a woman, since very few women serve in the armed forces. Or the age-old preference for men as administrators may mean that in a public agency crowded with women at the lower levels, the choice of men to be promoted is very limited. This means that superior women may have to work under the direction of less able men. Then too, the top officials in public agencies—the men and women who are heads of such departments as the Department of Health, Education, and Welfare—are political appointees, likely to lose their positions with each change of administration. They may be highly qualified people, or they may have been appointed without regard to their ability, solely for political reasons. This political patronage means that a successful candidate for public office must find at least a few important posts for his supporters. Inevitably, too, he is under pressure to appoint at least one person from some poorly represented section of the country or group in the population. So again a person who may or may not be capable gets the appointment.

In the United States today there are pressures for representation by regions, by religious groups, and by minorities—at least one woman or one prominent Negro American on some advisory council, for example. It also means emphasis on some of the newer nationality groups, such as Franco-Americans or Puerto Ricans or Mexicans. When the protesting group is widely dispersed over the country or within a state, the pressure may be brought to bear on the President or on the governor of a state. When the issue concerns a group that is localized, as Polish-Americans are in Detroit, Chicago, Gary, or Buffalo, all members of this minority, wherever they are, may be alerted to the problem through their national associations, but their vote is usually more important at local and state levels. So, dispersed special interest pressure groups balance regional groups.

In new countries, this is often called tribalism, or is presented as the behavior of one religious bloc against a properly constituted representative government. Americans, who see such behavior as political on a much wider scale, often fail to recognize that the new countries are dealing with group problems which, when the groups involved are localized in one part of the country, may mean the threat of possible civil war or the disruption of newly formed alliances.

There is also the question of public criticism of the performance of public agencies. Every experiment made by a public agency is subject to criticism, some of it good and helpful, some of it coming out of ignorance and prejudice, some of it frankly and cynically political. If public agencies undertake research projects, these may be criticized on many grounds. For example, if a local agricultural experiment station, supported jointly by the federal government and the government of a state, does some research on the nutritional qualities of apples and comes up with the finding that the apples grown in the state where it is located are inferior nutritionally to the apples grown by rival apple growers on the other side of the continent, this is political dynamite, both at the state and at the national level. A research laboratory that was part of an independent, privately supported or endowed agency could probably have made the same finding without political consequences that might endanger the future of such research in many parts of the country.

The directors of the great space programs in which rockets and then men were hurtled into space, finally to orbit the planet, faced this same sort of problem. The first astronauts were all test pilots. In testing new planes, it was usual for one or perhaps several pilots to lose their lives. But this risk could not be taken with a government program. And there were also doubts about the program. The American people were exceedingly conscious of the tremendous cost of the undertaking, in which all taxpayers would have to share, and there were many who felt that such a vast sum of money would be better spent on schools or hospitals or on simply making life on earth better. So if the space program were to continue to receive public support, it could not fail in the one unforgivable way, the death of an astronaut in space. Mechanical failure might result in public humiliation if a satellite failed to get off the launching pad or a rocket failed to reach the moon, but the life of the astronaut must come first. Here is a point on which public opinion remains adamant.

Private agencies can experiment with programs that have not yet received public acceptance—methods of treating illness that are still experimental, forms of education that are controversial. On a small scale, with a small group of people who are working on a program only because they believe in what they are doing, all kinds of ideas and experiments can be tried. Yet, if such projects are to succeed on a public scale, they must be so soundly conceived that they continue to operate long after the special enthusiasm and dedication of the people who first worked on them has been withdrawn.

So all over the United States, groups of enthusiastic parents start private schools for their children and the children of their neighbors and friends. These may be schools where gifted children will be free from restraint, schools where retarded children can learn at their own pace, schools where deaf or blind children will be taught by new methods, schools where children will start reading when they are two years old or not until they are eight, schools where small children will learn the principles of science, and schools where carefully selected representatives of all the different races and religions in the community will mingle.

Such schools take tremendous effort and the sacrifice of work and money, usually from young parents who have few resources. Many of them survive only a few years, but, in the meantime, some of the experimentation succeeds and becomes part of the educational wealth of the country—a child who went to the School of Organic Education in Fairhope, Alabama, in 1927, becomes responsible for new methods of teaching teachers of small children in 1964; a boy who went to a private progressive school at Croton-on-Hudson in 1940 is inventing new methods of teaching mathematics to first graders in 1959. And many of the innovations made in these little schools, like unscrewing the desks and giving the children chairs which can be moved about and grouped in different ways, a very simple idea but a new one, pass into the public schools.

Private organizations provide alternative ways of doing things: at least one private school in a community where you can send your child if the public school is totally unsuited to his needs; an agency in town that can care for cases of destitution so complicated that no public agency is equipped to handle them—a family, for instance, that has moved continually, a family in which the parents are citizens of different countries and the children were born in different states. All the way from the small town to the national capital, private agencies can—and do—do things that public agencies cannot do.

It is the essence of the American system that there should be alternatives, different places to go for help, and no regulations that restrict the individual to one source of relief, one kind of school, one church, or one political party. A mixed system, in which private, voluntary agencies are encouraged, seems a good way to ensure such freedom. It may sometimes also mean the freedom to have no form of some necessary service, in contrast to an orderly system in which all services are provided by the community and publicly financed. Towns may lack essential services ordinarily provided by private industry, and the institutions usually provided by private philanthropy may simply not be there. A city dependent upon privately operated trains and buses and airplanes may find itself almost isolated for lack of transportation. A mother with an emotionally disturbed child may find no mental health clinic within fifty miles.

These are the prices that are paid while Americans argue, and learn, about which should be private and which should be public responsibilities. And in order to make a responsibility public, they often have to go outside of the local community. If counseling services for all school children are necessary, then there must be state funds to supplement local support. If blind children are to be equally well cared for in every state, there must be a federal program. At no level of government in the United States does the higher authority order the more local authority to do something without helping to provide the means for doing it.

This may mean that a state permits a city to float a bond issue to build a new school or increases its appropriation to that community for the purpose. It may mean that the federal government pays, in whole or in part, for programs to provide relief for people who have residency in no state and claims on no local community. The principle still survives that the man who "pays the piper," in this case the government agency, "calls the tune," that those who chiefly support it have the right to insist on how a program goes. Ultimately, when an issue becomes deep enough and the local communities and the individual states are unable to deal with it, like social security, old age assistance, the care of dependent children, civil rights, construction of adequate hospitals, then the federal government, using the taxes paid by citizens in every part of the country, must step in.

But again at the national level, the private associations come into the picture. Whenever a new piece of legislation is contemplated that has nationwide significance, voluntary associations play a vital part in the preparation of it. Their board and staff members become part of the apparatus by which it is shaped, advising with officials of the federal agencies concerned and testifying before congressional committees studying bills as submitted to Congress. Often action goes from private to public agencies and back to private agencies again.

This happened in the antipoverty program launched in 1964. The need was initially highlighted by private organizations, such as the Council of the Southern Mountains, Incorporated, working in economically and socially depressed areas. Deeply concerned about the conditions revealed, President Johnson has made the abolition of poverty one of the major goals of his Administration, and the Congress appropriates funds for a program to work toward this objective. These funds, drawn from taxes paid to the national government, are channeled to communities through local agencies. Any community or organization, public or private, can present a plan for a project to reduce poverty and apply for money in accordance with the provisions of the congressional acts authorizing the antipoverty program.

This means that a city council, a board of education, a voluntary organization such as the Young Women's Christian Association, or a private or public educational institution, an industrial organization, or a labor union may submit a proposal and ask for a grant. Not all requests will be approved, but each one will be carefully considered by a review board made up of highly qualified people. Two of the communities described in chapter five of this book have received help of this kind: Guadalupe, Arizona, for a job training and retraining program; North Philadelphia, Pennsylvania, through contributions to the Opportunities Industrialization Center. There will be hundreds of other projects in other places: experiments in better education for children from underprivileged homes, efforts to train youngsters who have dropped out of school too early to be ready to work in the complicated economy of modern cities, counseling and classes and other services for girls who have married too young to be able to cope with babies and small children without help.

This, then, is the way that public action on a national problem is raised to the national level and brought to the attention of the public, and that funds are fed back so that local autonomy and local loyalties can come into play. Private business enterprise in America is inextricably combined with dependence upon governmental help, through subsidies and the making of contracts for services to be rendered; and in the field of private enterprise in good works, this is becoming increasingly so. The right to organize to carry out purposes held to be true and good, no matter how specialized, how starry-eyed or impractical the aims may appear to be, is one of the specially cherished aspects of American life.

X Four National Organizations

Exactly how many national organizations there are in the United States at any given time no one ever knows. The 1964 *Encyclopedia of American Associations* listed some 8,500, but even as this directory was being compiled the total was changing. Every year a number of new, national, voluntary organizations are formed, and a number go out of existence, their tasks accomplished or their money spent.

Although all of these societies and associations and federations have similar patterns of organization, each has its own special reason for being, its own objectives, its own ways of working, its own individuality. Each makes a contribution to American life that no other group can duplicate. Someday perhaps someone will write a history of the American people in terms of the organizations they have formed, beginning with the Pilgrim colony. For the United States owes its existence to groups of people who have been able to do together what no one person could ever have accomplished alone. The following descriptions of four currently active national organizations show some of the important ways in which voluntary associations contribute to American community life.

THE NATIONAL ASSOCIATION FOR RETARDED CHILDREN | Parents Organize on Behalf of Their Children

John is a winsome five-year-old, healthy physically, but mentally retarded. He is affectionate but independent, inquisitive but a very slow learner, destructive, and a runaway. One day, John followed two older boys from next door into a nearby wood while his ever-watchful mother was answering the telephone. When John was finally returned to his home by a policeman, after a long, anxious search, the mother of the two older boys scolded them severely. John's mother hurried across the lawn.

"Please don't punish them," she said to her neighbor. "John is my responsibility. It was not their fault."

"No," said the neighbor, her eyes full of tears, "he's *not* just your responsibility. He's the responsibility of *all of us,* and these two boys of mine have got to learn that. He belongs to this community, and we're *all* helping you look after him."

This true story is a touching example of changing American attitudes toward mental retardation. Much of the credit for this change is due to the National Association for Retarded Children (NARC), a parent-inspired, voluntary organization devoted to improving the welfare of the mentally retarded. It was founded in Minneapolis, Minnesota, in September, 1950, by forty people, mostly parents, representing local associations for retarded children in thirteen states. From this meeting came the present federation, which now has an individual membership of more than 100,000, more than 1,000 state and local member units scattered through all of the fifty states, and state federations in forty-nine states and the District of Columbia. More important than its size is the influence this organization has had and is having on the shaping of programs and policies relating to the diagnosis, care, training, and education of mentally retarded children and on research into the causes, prevention, and treatment of mental deficiency.

Why did this very successful, parent-initiated, parent-led association emerge when it did? "To every thing there is a season, and a time to every purpose under the heaven" (Ecclesiastes 3:1). In 1950 the time had come to do something decisive for the mentally retarded in the United States.

The time was right for four important reasons: (1) The lack of public school classes and other community facilities to help parents care for mentally defective children had become acute. (2) The American people had learned about, and were ashamed of, horrible conditions in many state institutions for the mentally incompetent, due to overcrowding and understaffing. (3) Parents of mentally retarded children were helping prepare for a great national congress—the mid-century White House Conference on Children and Youth—and knew that they would have an opportunity to present their case to the American people at this meeting if they were organized and ready, as a group. (4) There were indications that Congress might provide funds to meet the special needs of mentally retarded children within the framework of programs already being carried on by such government agencies as the Office of Education and the Children's Bureau, if the public would support such legislation.

So, the National Association for Retarded Children was formed in 1950 and went immediately to work. It had just two main objectives in the beginning: to arouse the public to the seriousness of the mental retardation problem, its size and its cost, measured in terms of money and human frustration; and to get adequate day schools and proper residential treatment centers for retarded children.

To accomplish its first objective, NARC has continuously emphasized the statistical side of the problem. At any given time, the mentally retarded group in the United States includes between 3 and 4 percent of the population. According to the best obtainable estimates, there are now nearly six million people in this group, about two and one half million of them children and youth under twenty years of age. It is difficult to obtain more exact figures than these, for, prompted by feelings of guilt and embarrassment, many parents hide their mentally defective youngsters. Since at least two million of the under-twenty retardates are in some degree educable, many of them can become wholly or partly self-sufficient adults if they receive proper training in time. An estimated 150,000 are in the moderately retarded group, capable of learning to attend to their personal needs and able to do useful work in the business world under the right supervision or in special sheltered workshop situations.

These statistics represent a problem that should not have been ignored so long. The figures add up to an appalling waste of human energy and potential. The cost to American taxpayers, as long as the mentally retarded are neglected, is fantastic. It includes charges to the public for the support of schools, custodial institutions, and related social services that amount to over half a billion dollars a year, a sum at least matched by the costs borne by families. Indirect costs, especially the loss to the economy of the output of people who could do paid work but have few opportunities for employment, are estimated at about five billion dollars a year. There is no possible way of calculating the cost in terms of human suffering.

The program of NARC, begun with a drive for classes and treatment centers, now has many facets, all interrelated: diagnostic and treatment clinics; home visiting programs organized by clinics and health and welfare organizations to help parents struggling with especially difficult cases; discussion groups and classes for parents; day care services; nursery schools where parents assist and learn under the supervision of trained teachers how to handle their retarded children; special classes and training centers for children of school age; special recreational facilities; vocational training and job placement services for subnormal adults; homes where the more severely retarded can live for a time under professional observation, to determine whether they can live best at home, in a community residential center, or in an institution; halfway houses to make the transition from institution to home less abrupt; residential centers for short- or long-term treatment; religious education; legal protection and guardianship; and, perhaps most important of all, research into the causes of the many different kinds of mental retardation.

Until recently, there were so few studies of mental retardation that very little was positively known about its etiology; most people considered it a hopeless condition. Now research in the biological sciences has revealed at least two hundred probable causes, a few of which can be removed if detected soon enough. Today, research scientists, educators, physicians, psychiatists, and psychologists have literally doubled their efforts to gain the knowledge so desperately needed to prevent and treat more successfully the complex condition known by the very loose and general term of mental retardation. Now research is already showing that many children who behave as though they were mentally retarded are, in fact, potentially normal in intelligence. Some are children from disadvantaged homes where they have little or none of the stimulation essential for the awakening of a child's mind—no training in self-control, no encouragement when speech is being formed, no songs or stories to help a child learn to express himself in the idioms of American culture. Other youngsters who seem retarded may be partially or totally deaf, or only semisighted. To these deprived but not mentally defective children, the

National Association for Retarded Children has a mission of liberation, too.

Because progress in any preventive or remedial program depends on the closest possible collaboration among all of the professions and all of the public and private agencies concerned in any way with mental retardation, NARC spends a great deal of time arranging interdisciplinary conferences and consultations. It recently convened the first American Inter-Organization Conference on Mental Retardation and helped plan a substantial number of interdisciplinary research and demonstration projects. Since it helped to obtain the federal government funds now available to states for the benefit of the mentally retarded, the association is deeply involved with both public and private agencies in the development of state and local projects that qualify for government aid. It is especially interested in helping universities to develop all the facilities necessary for the well-rounded training of specialists serving the mentally retarded: doctors, nurses, social workers, teachers, attendants, and others.

With all its responsibilities, NARC finds time to publish a bimonthly newspaper for parents, *Children Limited*, which is outstanding for its warmth and friendliness and for the extraordinary amount of practical information it contains about new developments in the study, care, and training of mentally handicapped children. *Children Limited* is circulated to the entire membership of the association and is an interesting example of the kind of special-interest magazine that many organizations issue to keep their members in touch with what is going on in their particular fields of interest and to tell other readers what the program it represents is all about.

It would be hard to find a better illustration of private initiative, of private individuals taking the lead in a massive attack on a nationwide problem, than the National Association for Retarded Children. To each of the parents who helped to form this organization, the problem was at first a very personal one—in this family, a beautiful baby showing no sign of intelligence; in that home, a gangling adolescent with the mind of a six-year-old. These mothers and fathers worked at first for the sake of their own children, for the relief of their own pain. But as they worked they learned that mental retardation is a matter of national concern, not just a private heartache. With this new insight, they broadened their objectives. Other people joined them in their search for causes and new methods of prevention and treatment. Money came from many sources. The individual initiative of parents became community initiative; community initiative stimulated state and national action. In fifteen short years, the NARC program, starting modestly in 1950, has become one of the most comprehensive efforts to solve an insidious social problem in the history of the United States.

RURITAN NATIONAL | Bridge Between Town and Country

In contrast with the National Association for Retarded Children, Ruritan National is a small, little-known organization. But it is an important one because it works effectively at the very roots of a problem that causes concern, not only in the United States, but in many other parts of the world: a lack of understanding between farmers with small holdings and the business and professional people in nearby urban centers.

In the late 1920's, there was growing friction between townspeople and farmers in Nansemond, a rural county in southeastern Virginia. The feelings of estrangement were natural (although regrettable) because urban and rural ways of life there were so different. For example, it is noon in Holland, a Nansemond County village; the 12 o'clock whistle blows at a warehouse on the edge of town. George Brown, president of the local bank, looks at the clock on his office wall, puts away the paper he has just signed—perhaps an application for a loan from Farmer Jones—walks across the street to the hotel, and immediately is one of a jolly group of friends gathered for their weekly service club luncheon.

Farmer Jones hears the noon whistle too. But he, dressed in overalls, is working in a field. He leaves his cultivator, goes to his house, washes his hands at the kitchen sink, and eats dinner with his family. On his way back to work, he may say to himself, if he happens to think of it, "This is Rotary-Kiwanis day. I'd like to be able to get off once a week to go to a meeting like that. I never heard of any farmers belonging to Rotary-Kiwanis. Maybe it's just as well they don't ask us to join. We don't usually see things the way they do."

But farmers and business and professional men did get together in Holland in 1928, with the help of two people. One was J. J. Gwaltney, a teacher of vocational agriculture at the Holland high school; the other, Tom V. Downing, district supervisor of vocational agriculture in eastern Virginia. Gwaltney was sensitive to the rural-urban frictions in his area, but his immediate concern was his work as an agriculture teacher. He had as yet found no satisfactory way of sharing with the farmers in his region the new information about crops and farming methods that came to him in a steady stream from many sources. To be sure, he was holding evening classes; a few men came faithfully to these, but the meetings were often not well attended.

Gwaltney could understand why it was hard for farmers to come out at night. These men were peanut growers and worked in the fields from dawn until dark from March to December. In the winter months they worked just as hard mending fences, repairing machinery, and getting ready for spring planting. They were too tired and too busy at all times of the year to come regularly to classes at night, no matter how much they wanted the help they might get from instruction.

Among other possibilities, Gwaltney considered monthly luncheon meetings. Perhaps, he thought, we might organize a club for farmers. Men who understood the farming problems of the county might be asked to speak. There might even be joint meetings, occasionally, with Holland service clubs, so that townsmen and farmers could become better acquainted. Some of Gwaltney's friends discouraged this idea. Farmers, they said, would always be too pressed for time to get away in the middle of the day. "Besides," they added, "farmers won't pay to eat a meal away from home when home-cooked food tastes better and costs less than food served in public eating places." Still, Gwaltney decided to talk over the club idea with his supervisor the next time Downing came to Holland.

Downing, meanwhile, was worrying about other matters besides agriculture education and rural-urban frictions in Nansemond County; he wanted to see the people in that county organize to solve a whole list of community problems. The county needed recreational facilities, better schools, better health and welfare services, and a clean-up and beautification campaign. He knew that many previous attempts at rural community organization had failed. But were the difficulties really insurmountable? He found the answer to this question one day when he happened to be in Norfolk, Virginia, and was invited to a noon meeting at the Naval YMCA. To his surprise, he learned that he was being entertained by a farmers' service club. As he had suspected, the notion that farmers would not support such an organization was a myth. Encouraged by what he had seen in Norfolk, Downing went on to Holland, where he and J. J. Gwaltney worked out a plan for a town-and-country supper club to serve the needs of the Holland area.

This plan was the beginning of Ruritan. It provided for supper meetings, quarterly dues payable in advance, membership by invitation, a lively program at each meeting. A meeting was called in Holland on April 18, 1928, for the purpose of forming the new organization, one "in which town and country, together, might practice the art of fellowship and understanding." The nucleus of the first group was the teacher's evening class, with business and professional men from Holland also invited. (The name chosen for the new club, *Ruritan*, was coined from the Latin *rus*, country, and *urbs*, city.) Additional clubs were formed in rapid succession, first in other parts of Virginia, then in neighboring states. Four clubs joined together in 1930 to make Ruritan a national organization; the first national convention was held in Suffolk, the county seat of Nansemond County, Virginia, in early 1932, with some ten clubs sending representatives. There are now 1,000 Ruritan clubs in nineteen states, with approximately 32,000 members. The average monthly attendance is close to 80 percent.

The purpose of Ruritan is "to bring a closer social union between the farmers and the business and professional men of a community in order to make it a better place in which to live." The program through which this purpose is carried out has a distinctly local flavor. Members of Ruritan organize community centers, usually buying the property and putting up the buildings themselves; in mountainous counties, this may mean leveling rock ledges, digging ditches for piping water, laying out roads and driveways. They gather to help when disaster strikes a farm. They also perform community chores, such as taking care of historical landmarks, putting up street signs, donating equipment for hospitals, and building roadside parks.

On another level of activity, Ruritan takes responsibility for interpreting new state and federal legislation of interest to members, conducts forestry classes, establishes volunteer fire departments, and develops recreational areas. The clubs raise money in countless ways, but mostly by providing the kinds of entertainment that people on farms and in small country towns have always enjoyed: fairs, cattle and horse shows, minstrel shows, barn dances, fish fries, beauty contests, barbecues, auctions, and stock sales. Part of this money is used to send promising local boys and girls away to college. Committees investigate and report on conditions and needs in their home communities. Local Ruritan clubs then decide what they can do to help, either by work members can do or through cooperation with other local organizations.

Because Ruritan is essentially a rural organization, there is a practical, neighborly quality about its work. But its outlook is not provincial. At the monthly supper meetings, men of many occupations sit down together: farmers, service station men, teachers, merchants, doctors, postal employees, lumbermen, lawyers, public officials, preachers, millers, railroaders, restaurant owners, salesmen, garage operators, and newspapermen. The members sing together, enjoy the entertainment provided, talk frankly about matters of common concern, and listen to speakers who not only bring accurate information about programs affecting urban and rural communities, such as government farm subsidies and social security, but also discuss national and international issues of the day.

"By bringing together citizens of purpose and energy," former President Eisenhower once said, "Ruritan has built an organization of strength to the rural community. With the twin objectives of progress and neighborly service, it provides inspiration to build a better life for all."

THE NATIONAL CONGRESS OF PARENTS AND TEACHERS | A Strong Partnership

The best way to understand that essentially American institution known as the Parent-Teacher Association is to visit a public elementary school on an evening in early autumn, soon after school has started for the year, when a local PTA is meeting. The doors of the building are open, and lights shine from the windows. Parents are arriving singly and in little knots of four or five; a few fathers stop on the steps for a last cigarette. Inside the school, young mothers hover over the tea tables set up in the front of the auditorium, anxiously checking to make sure that the refreshments are nicely arranged and that nothing has been forgotten. Other mothers and fathers are wandering up and down the corridors looking at exhibits of the children's work mounted on the walls. Teachers are talking with parents in their classrooms, and children who will take part in a play to be given later at the meeting are giggling in the anteroom behind the stage.

After the visiting and the informal parent-teacher conferences are over, the meeting begins with discussions of uncompleted old business, moves on to new business, then to the entertainment. If the group has taken action about something, committees are appointed to take the matter in hand. The meeting ends early; fathers and mothers collect their youngsters, say good-night to their friends, and disappear into the night. One by one the lights in the windows go out, the front door is locked, and the building is in darkness.

A community would indeed be in darkness of another kind if no such meetings were ever held in its schools, for this would mean that the two agencies most responsible for the education and guidance of young children, the home and the school, would not be in contact. It would also mean that the parents of that community would be deprived of the leadership of the national organization to which all local PTA's belong.

This parent organization is the National Congress of Parents and Teachers. It has almost twelve million members in the United States and many friends around the world. Its purposes are: "To promote the welfare of children and youth in home, school, church, and community; to raise the standards of home life; to secure adequate laws for the care and protection of children and youth; to bring the home and the school into closer relationship, so that parents and teachers may cooperate intelligently in the training of the child; and to develop between educators and the general public such united efforts as will secure for every child the highest advantages of physical, mental, social, and spiritual education."[1] It works closely with educational authorities at local, state, and national levels, in a supporting role. Except in very unusual circumstances, it does not concern itself with responsibilities that rightly belong to professional educators, such as curriculum-making, teaching methods, or teacher qualifications.

The national PTA is one of the few organizations in the United States that started as a national organization and then spread to local communities throughout the land. It was founded in 1897 by a Washington, D. C., housewife, Mrs. Alice McLellan Birney. Mrs. Birney, like so many other women at the close of the nineteenth century, was deeply troubled about what was happening to children in communities too poor or too indifferent to provide the right conditions for wholesome child growth and development. One day when she was wondering what she could do to help secure a healthy, happy childhood for all American youngsters, Mrs. Birney suddenly had an idea.

"Think of the power and prestige of the United States Congress," she said to some friends. "Why couldn't we have a Congress of Mothers? One mother alone can do very little to change conditions that affect the health and welfare of her children, but thousands of mothers working together could accomplish almost anything. Let us call the mothers of the United States to a congress, here, in the nation's capital, to make known their problems, to tell about the hopes they have for their children and the obstacles that seem to stand in the way of realiz-

---

[1] National Congress of Parents and Teachers, *The Parent-Teacher Organization: Its Origins and Development* (Chicago: The Congress, 1944), page 184.

ing these hopes. Surely some of their concerns could be translated into programs of social and legislative action."[2]

Mrs. Birney's enthusiasm was contagious. Her friends were impressed with her proposal and offered to help organize such a congress. With this assurance of support, Mrs. Birney and her volunteers began to visit women's groups wherever they could find them. They were particularly anxious to reach mothers in rural communities. When roads were too rough and hills too steep for carriages, they went on horseback or on foot. The wife of a United States senator, Mrs. Phoebe Apperson Hearst, was one of this early group. She gave not only of her time and energy but supplied generous financial assistance. In fact, Mrs. Birney and Mrs. Hearst were the actual founders of the organization.

The first Congress of Mothers turned out to be an amazing success. To the surprise of everyone concerned, two thousand women and a few men streamed into Washington to attend the meeting, a far larger number than had been expected. Most of these people were already sensitive to the needs of children and, in their own ways, were trying to meet these needs. They welcomed the opportunity to multiply their efforts through a dynamic, new organization. Today more than one third of the 12 million members are men. Teachers have been officially included in the organization since 1908, when it became the National Congress of Parents and Teachers.

The structure of this huge association is simple. There are some 47,000 local Parent-Teacher Associations, each one a self-governing unit. In every state of the Union and the District of Columbia, there is a branch of the national organization which serves as a connecting link between the national organization and the PTA members in the local groups within its particular geographical area. Thus every PTA member belongs not

---

[2] Harry and Bonaro Overstreet, *Where Children Come First: A Study of the P.T.A. Idea* (Chicago, The National Congress of Parents and Teachers, 1949) p. 41, paraphrased.

only to his own Parent-Teacher Association but also to the state branch and to the national organization.

The National Congress of Parents and Teachers has the usual national, state, and local officers. It has an unusually large number of standing committees, however, through which its very extensive and varied program is carried on. Among these standing committees are committees on audio-visual services, character and spiritual education, citizenship, cooperation with the colleges, cultural arts, exceptional children, health, high school service, international relations, juvenile protection, legislation, membership, mental health, National Congress publications, *The PTA Magazine*, parent and family life education, preschool service, program service, publicity, reading and library service, recreation, rural service, safety, and school education.

The PTA Magazine, published since 1906, serves the Congress in a number of important ways. Read and discussed in every local PTA, it unites this vast membership in spirit, purpose, and action. It provides reliable information on subjects of interest to both parents and teachers, and serves as a study guide for courses sponsored by local associations for parents of preschool and school-age children and adolescents. For example, articles in a recent issue, especially planned for groups studying adolescence, discussed subjects of current concern to teen-agers and their parents: "Citizens Now—Voters Soon," "The Morals of a Teen," and "Social Graces and Disgraces," the latter dealing with the very controversial subject of teen-age manners. A feature story, "Reflections on Poverty in America," in this same issue, shows how closely the PTA relates its work to national affairs.

It is hard to believe that any organization could grow from 2,000 to 12 million members in 70 years, yet this one did, fulfilling the highest hopes of the women who founded it. Mothers and fathers in the smallest local association in the smallest school in the smallest hamlet in the United States can now state their childrearing problems, knowing that what they have to say will be heard by their state and national officers and, with other concerns expressed by parents, will be translated into the ongoing program of the Congress.

Although the National Congress of Parents and Teachers is politically nonpartisan, it is not neutral when the welfare of children and families is threatened, and it translates the hopes and anxieties of parents into social and legislative action when the need arises. It works through and with other like-minded organizations and government agencies "to promote opportunities for children and youth to realize their full potential for a creative life in freedom and dignity"—the theme of the 1960 White House Conference on Children and Youth, which the National Congress helped to organize.

NATIONAL TRAVELERS AID ASSOCIATION | A Modern Good Samaritan

In 1851, the covered wagons were heading toward the glitter of freshly discovered gold in California. Although many men went alone into the mountains with their picks and shovels, thousands of families started from the East Coast in the rush for treasure, and for many of these, the city of St. Louis, Missouri, was the journey's end. Money gave out, wagons broke down, mothers or fathers or children fell ill and could not go on. The mayor of St. Louis was so distressed by the plight of these stranded people that he gave a great deal of his own money to help them and, when he died, left more than half a million dollars to be used to assist them. It was with these funds that the first Travelers Aid program was started.

In the next fifty years, many organizations for helping travelers in trouble were formed in different parts of the United States. By 1905, more than two hundred local groups had taken the name Travelers Aid Society, a name then used in England by such agencies. In the early days of the American movement, much of the local support came from the Young Women's Christian Association and other organizations dedicated to the protection of young girls and women leaving home to take part in the nation's great industrial development.

The first step toward the formation of a national federation of local, autonomous groups came in 1911, when the New York Travelers Aid Society set up a Department of National Cooperation. After World War I, the work of the Travelers Aid was greatly increased as thousands of European refugees came to the United States looking for safety and liberty. During this period, too, the service had to be geared to meet the needs of an increasing number of travelers who had personal problems to resolve in addition to the exigencies of travel. The peak of the demand for help with these many different kinds of emergencies came during the depression of the 1930's, when seemingly endless numbers of people, unemployed and without funds, wandered about the country looking for work.

During World War II, the Travelers Aid Association became one of six organizations providing hospitality and other kinds of aid to men in the armed forces through a new cooperative agency, the United Service Organization (USO). As much and sometimes more in need of assistance than the enlisted men and officers were their families. Volunteers who worked as members of Travelers Aid in these war years will never forget the exhausted young mothers with fretful babies and crying toddlers, sitting all night in public rest rooms, waiting for buses to take them to their husbands in army camps all over the United States. Their weariness and pain were in no way comparable to the suffering of refugees in many parts of the world at that time, but these wives and children—the dependents of men in military service—were in misery and needed help. So, too, did the families of soldiers and defense workers in the Korean War, soon to follow World War II.

In 1960, the National Travelers Aid Association,

headquartered in New York, took a fresh, long look at its program in the light of changing economic and social conditions in the United States and changing needs for service to travelers. New forms of transportation had changed traveling habits and created new traveling problems. Travelers Aid was now meeting persons in distress at airports as well as in bus terminals and railroad stations. But the majority of calls for aid were now coming from stranded motorists. A survey in 1960 showed that 70 percent of Americans then traveled by car; the next largest number by bus. These two groups together accounted for more than 50 percent of the cases handled by Travelers Aid in that year, and still do.

Stranded motorists are a major challenge which the Travelers Aid Association is meeting with the flexibility and inventiveness that have characterized its work from the beginning. When an old car breaks down with a family in it, the father or an older child usually tries to reach the nearest service station. The station operator is then likely to call the highway police. An average of ten thousand such calls are received annually by service station men and the police in the Pittsburgh, Pennsylvannia, area alone.

Many of the people in trouble on the roads today are migrant laborers hunting for jobs, so the trade unions are concerned about them. Together, the Travelers Aid Association and the AFL-CIO are trying to find the best way of getting help quickly to those who need it. The unions have provided mobile units for Travelers Aid workers, who use them as offices on wheels. These units are equipped with two-way radio systems and telephones. When a highway patrolman receives a call for assistance, he relays it to the Travelers Aid mobile unit. The unit speeds to the rescue, gives emergency aid, and then, if the family wishes, begins an intensive effort to help solve more basic problems. Many of these families would not be on the road if they had been able to meet the demands of community life. With the right sort of guidance, they can often settle somewhere and rehabilitate themselves. One of the mobile units is in southern New Jersey, the other in California. If this plan succeeds, there will be other units.

Perhaps in a country where people move about as much as they do in the United States, the Travelers Aid Association will sometime change its time-honored name to Traveling Aid Association. In any event, it will certainly adapt its program to meet any future changes in transportation, as it has done to meet such changes in the past. Someday, no doubt, a little spacemobile bearing the familiar Travelers Aid emblem will come rushing to the aid of travelers in trouble in outer space.

Although their purposes and programs are different, each of the four organizations just described has followed the typical American pattern of group development. Someone had an idea and shared it with a few other interested persons. These people decided to give life to the idea by forming an association. They announced plans for the new organization, clearly stating its aims. They invited others to join. They held a founding meeting.

At this point, the entire membership took responsibility for the venture. Committees were elected or appointed to perform specific tasks. Basic documents, such as a constitution, were prepared to anchor the program of work to the values and purposes of the association. Various special publications were issued to keep channels of communication open between officers and members and among members. As the organization grew, it continually evaluated its activities, changing its policies and services, if necessary, to meet changing needs in its chosen field of work. Close and friendly relationships were developed with other community, state, and national organizations and agencies, public and private.

Some of the developments, over the years, in each of these four organizations have been unexpected. Not one of them started out to be international, but sooner rather than later, each one began to reach out across political and cultural boundary lines to like-minded people in other countries. Friendly approaches drew warm responses from individuals of many nationalities, who used *their* initiative to found their own chapters or branches of transnational groups in which they were interested. In this way, these four and many other American organizations have helped to forge bonds of mutual understanding and esteem between people in many different parts of the world.

XI

Leadership in an Open Society

American community life is far more dependent upon voluntary effort than is life in many other parts of the world where centralized government planning or traditional village, town, or tribal leadership either keeps things moving along established lines or takes charge of innovations that have been decided elsewhere. But the smallest towns and the largest cities in the United States will quite literally wither and decay without continuous voluntary efforts on the part of many people to keep them going, make them change, correct abuses, develop new possibilities, and take part in relevant programs that have been started elsewhere.

Where there are no patterns or channels for such activity, streets become untidy, signs swing loose on their hinges, parks are neglected, sidewalks crack, trees are not planted, rubbish piles up on empty lots, and deserted buildings become eyesores. The schools run down, the teaching deteriorates, adolescents with nothing to do get into mischief and then serious trouble, the citizens' health is impaired, children's teeth are neglected, there are fewer immunizations against disease, the chronically ill go unvisited, and lonely old people are left to fend for themselves.

The fact is that there are not sufficient government mechanisms to accomplish all the tasks of simple community maintenance. Keeping a town or city running properly is like keeping a house in order. It means keeping roofs and buildings painted and in repair, as good householders do; keeping all the people under the home roofs fed and cared for, as good mothers do. The government, no matter how complicated it may become in a city, let us say, of a million people, is never expected to do the whole job. Even when a local community is too poor or too leaderless or too reactionary to get some needed task performed and a cry goes up for the state or a federal agency to step into the situation, no one assumes that a government program will work on its own.

Furthermore, in cities there is never enough coordination, either of government or of voluntary agencies, to ensure that the whole city will be in good shape at any given time, let alone stay in good shape and move with the times. In all cities there will be patches of poverty and neglect, sections where there are no local voluntary groups to keep an eye on things. No citywide programs reach into all the back streets, into places down by the docks, along the railroad tracks, or by the riverbank.

Even when there are city-wide programs for a good civic purpose—for instance, a clean-up campaign that puts trash cans at street corners and then arranges for a proper garbage collection service; a drive to get every school child X-rayed; a drive to get every healthy adult to donate blood to the Red Cross blood bank—still, without local organization the area will languish, the trash cans will go unused, the garbage collection will falter, the X-ray program will peter out. In very large cities, streets or areas of a very few blocks may show striking differences in upkeep, in safety, in the care of children, depending upon the strength and the activity of local political and other public-spirited organizations. This is the reason why Americans periodically "discover" that some group —tenant farmers, new immigrants, migrant workers, out-of-school youth, the aged, the unemployed, Negro Americans, Mexican-Americans, American Indians—has fallen far below the standard of living most Americans, especially those who live in well-managed towns and suburbs, believe to be the American way of life.

The country is so big that when statistics are published showing how many cars or television sets or washing machines are sold each year, it is easy to feel that every American family must have, not one of each, but several. New cars crowd the main highways to such an extent that the occasional very old cars keep to the back roads and seldom appear on the big highways, except in times of mass migrations. The pictures of home life in mazazines, in advertisements, in movies, and on television always, or nearly always, show bright, shining, well-kept houses, trim, well-groomed men, pretty, well-dressed, manicured women, bright, cheerful, happy children. The house the family lives in is a new house, a good house, with a well-kept lawn; the car in the driveway is a new one.

Many Americans have come to confuse this storybook house with the average American home. So some American soldiers overseas, who may have come from slums or run-down, neglected little villages bypassed by time, will, in all honesty, describe these magazine dream houses and tell their friends that these are the kinds of homes Americans live in. These soldiers know their own homes are not like that, but they quite sincerely believe that almost all other American homes are. True, *their* parents are poor, *their* town is a miserable place, *their* part of the country has had bad luck for years, but *Americans* live well, their children go to good schools, and any man who wants a job can find one.

This optimistic, rosy-hued picture has been based, from the beginning, on the hopes of the early colonists, the efforts of the pioneers, who saw in their log cabins the well-built houses of smooth boards or bricks or stone that would soon replace them. The image is based, too, on the dreams of millions of nineteenth-century and early twentieth-century immigrants who believed that the streets of the country they were coming to were paved with gold. Although they were sorely disappointed, most of them did prosper far beyond the conditions in their native lands that had driven them to emigrate. It was those who were willing to work hard for a new way of life who came to the United States during its formative period; and their hard work counted, if not in their generation, then certainly in their children's generations. But to the dispossessed Indians and to the descendants of the African slaves brought here against their will, America did not seem a land of opportunity. One aspect of their tragedy was that for a long time people who knew how poor most of them were found it easy to rationalize that American Indian or Negro poverty was due to innate laziness or primitiveness.

It comes as a shock, then, when a new movement, a new campaign, or a political leader suddenly announces, and proves, that large numbers of Americans are living far below the standard of living expected for the country as a whole, lost, forgotten, sunk in poverty and despair. We experienced this in the social protest movements of earlier times; the fight for free schools led by one of the first labor unions; the settlement house movement, in which responsible, sometimes wealthy, but always compassionate, men and women moved into the slums to help immigrants huddled so closely together that their very numbers cut them off from pathways of escape. In the 1930's, there was the great upsurge of concern for small farmers in forgotten parts of the country, American citizens who barely scraped a living from poor or exhausted soil and were literally homeless, ruined by drought and an economic depression.

Today, in the antipoverty program, there is again a

massive campaign to bring to the attention of every American the plight of some 36 million fellow country-men whose present condition, in the midst of prosperity enjoyed by others, places them under the dividing line between poverty and plenty. The antipoverty program is intended to relieve human beings suffering from many different kinds of misfortunes and deprivations—the people living in backward parts of backward states where schools, roads, housing, and everything else is poor. The program is also intended to educate those who have had so little schooling that they are at a disadvantage in the modern world. It is planned to help those who grew up in city slums without the kind of training that would have enabled them to leave. The program is planned to help members of minority groups, particularly Negro Americans, and is intended to also reach the great mass of untrained young people who cannot find jobs because automation, through the introduction of new machinery, has reduced the number of available jobs for unskilled workers. Until these untrained young people get job training, they cannot qualify for the jobs that do exist.

Social movements like these have had a powerful influence on the development of American social ideals. Each movement has attacked a problem affecting the welfare of millions of people and made progress toward its solution. But in the long run, the fate of each community still lies in the hands of the people who live there. In times of emergency, the community may get massive help from outside; slowly the state or the federal government may take over some of the things the community once had to do entirely for itself. When the nation was founded, the new national government became responsible for defense, for a national currency, for traffic and commerce between the states.

Today, no activity is carried on in even the smallest town without possibilities of help, resources, and guidance from larger units, whether the people of the town are trying to found a local chapter of some national organization or trying to learn how to solve a local problem or trying to find a way to participate in a new nationwide public program. No road is built, even inside the town limits, that does not have to be coordinated with state and national road-building programs. No school, not even one founded by a tiny, local, new, religious community determined to educate its own children to follow in the footsteps of their elders, can be established and maintained without meeting certain requirements about hours and ages, school books, and square feet of space per child—rules established by the education department of its state government. Not even the smallest village lives unto itself alone.

But what the village or the town or the city or the state makes of its opportunities for help is still strictly a local matter. A state can go temporarily bankrupt and be unable to pay its civil servants. A city can get itself bogged down in a morass of debt, unfulfilled plans, half-dug subways, and unfinished schools. The majority of citizens in a small town can vote for years against a needed sewage disposal plant or a new water works; or stand out, recalcitrant and stubborn, against the incorporation of their town into the great city that has grown out and around it, even when this incorporation would be of benefit to them. The uncompromising sense of independence and autonomy that characterized the early colonists persists; its forms may change, but the spirit remains.

As the accounts of Tin Top, Waterford, North Philadelphia, and Guadalupe have shown, it takes leadership of a high quality to help a community change its pattern of organization, even if the new idea is attractive and practical and something a good many people want. It takes leadership of an even higher order to help a weak community find its strengths or to break through situations in which there is fear of trying new methods despite the fact that the old organizational forms are inadequate. But the curious thing about leadership in American communities is that it is of so many sorts and can be exercised by so many different kinds of people that there is no simple formula by which one can predict that "this town" or even a "town of this sort" will have good leadership. It is fairly easy, however, to describe the kind of town in which there is likely to be a lack of leadership.

If one looks at communities structurally, it is apparent that those with the largest number of institutions linking them with the wider world are also the ones that have the greatest reservoirs of leadership. The presence of a university or a college, of technical centers or research laboratories, of museums, art schools, historical societies, of regional offices of governmental and nongovernmental organizations is a promise that there will be available locally individuals who can take initiative and who will also know where to find necessary help outside the community. This is good, unless a town becomes overweighted with such people and turns into what is known as a college or university town or a research center. Then there may develop the kind of rift which used to be called "town and gown." Then antagonisms may grow, making the townspeople unwilling to use local technical or academic leadership.

Another problem arises when prominent political figures retire from public life, go back to their local communities and, because of their tremendous capacity to initiate and lead, become a burden rather than a help. They become a burden because they are just too powerful for so limited a sphere of action.

Then there is the case of the single industry, with great laboratories and complex public relationships, which finances great community improvements but by so doing paralyzes local initiative. In planning new towns, the need for centers of educated leadership is important, but the dangers also have to be kept in mind.

The town with many ongoing organizations and institutions will have many experienced, competent people who are used to sitting on committees, presiding at meetings, organizing luncheons and dinners, speaking in public, and persuading other people to cooperate. Such people are essential, but here again there are dangers. A town may have such a good supply of established leadership of this kind that presidencies and chairmanships are simply passed about within a small group of able people who are accustomed to working together and oppose any new leadership. When emergencies or unexpected opportunities arise, the old leadership may be more intent on keeping power than on really coping with the new situation.

Diversity of interests is undoubtedly the key to a community that can develop efficiently and use all kinds of people in all kinds of leadership positions so that leadership comes from many areas, such as industry, the academic and artistic sectors, religious groups, labor unions, and from the special ethnic groups that still feel themselves separate from the rest of the community. The more such sectors there are, the more leaders will be available. But, if a town is divided between labor and management, with all the other sectors playing subsidiary roles, it may well be that only two outstanding leaders are produced, the one who speaks for labor and the one who speaks for management.

If all the voluntary welfare agencies in a community are grouped according to the major religious auspices, Catholic, Jewish, and Protestant, then there will be places for leaders from each of these groups on coordinating councils; if any sector claims more than one place, others may feel under undue pressure. But as the problems which face the agencies multiply and change, a fourth group requiring representation may emerge in the community, labor unions, perhaps, or Negroes. This will mean more openings for leaders on committees or community councils, into which a series of able individuals can step.

A quite common practice is to have panel discussions in which representatives of different groups, sitting together on a platform at a public meeting, speak on behalf of their groups or interests. This is another way in which spokesmen with leadership possibilities are found. Finally, every organization affiliated with state and national and international organizations also provides positions for which able and competent people are needed, and as these are recruited, more leaders are discovered.

In a hierarchical society, where it was the duke or the squire or the chief on whom all leadership and initiative devolved, communities were sometimes fortunate and sometimes unfortunate in the leadership they had. There was almost nothing that the average citizen could do about it when the leadership was bad, except present petitions, introduce boycotts, riot—or flee if conditions became too intolerable. But wherever there is a structure which provides many positions but does not specify who must hold them (so that able people may be found for them, and able people may, themselves, look for places where they can lead), then here is a situation in which leadership capacity can be multiplied.

The word *leadership* is a term that is only applied, in America, as a term of approval. No matter how many adherents they temporarily attract, we do not say that programs of destructiveness and reaction are "led"; followers of a discredited prophet will be spoken of as "misled," "misguided," or "deluded." The German title Hitler took for himself, *Der Führer*, is now used to distinguish Nazi leadership from the kind of leadership characteristic of men like Franklin D. Roosevelt. On the other hand, those in the United States who did not accept President Roosevelt's aims and goals would not have used the word *leader* for him.

So when heroes and heroines are selected from the past to serve as models for American children, they will not all be accepted equally. In general, Americans speak of someone as a great leader or, more often still, say that he provided great leadership, if he advanced a cause to which they themselves are deeply committed. A new school building, for example, may have carved over its door the name of Horace Mann, a name known to few people outside the field of education. But the loyalty of particular segments of the population to particular leaders is so great that it is not difficult for a speaker in a political campaign to look up the heroes who will be dear to the hearts of some special audience and use them to establish rapport, to give those present a new sense of themselves as people in sympathy with each other and with him.

Only a few of these sectional leaders actually become national heroes. The name George Washington has almost universal evocatory power. Yet, beyond the fact that he is called the "Father of His Country," the actual personality of the man himself is very vaguely perceived. Abraham Lincoln's name, to which people respond with reverence throughout a large part of the nation, still has no such appeal for white Southerners in the states defeated in the Civil War. Very often it astonishes members of other countries who have focused their feelings of appreciation on some well-known American political figure, such as former Presidents Wilson, Franklin Roosevelt, or Kennedy, to find that such men exercised little or no charismatic leadership over many of the American people while they were living.

Extravagant partisanship there is, and in time of emergency, a willingness to trust and carry out a President's plan; but even in a crisis, the ability to stand aside and criticize is very strong. Americans are not a people trained to give uncritical love and affection to either their Presidents or their parents. Having inherited the Protestant tradition, which stresses the right of every man to interpret the word of God for himself, they are everlastingly looking for proof—facts to support any claim that is made. This does not mean that they are necessarily better at recognizing actual facts, but it does mean that they are wary of giving to any mere human being any kind of unconditional assent. There is a distrust of strong leadership, especially if it is joined with a bid for power.

And the man who seeks power in public office because he wants to change the world for the better is more distrusted than the man who seeks public office simply because he has made politics his career. Only after he has been somewhat idealized by death do people forget the political tactics that brought the office seeker to power.

Within a community, those whom the press speaks of as "community leaders" are those who have devoted themselves, imaginatively or unimaginatively, to public service. This includes serving in government, where there are unpaid, honorific jobs to which busy, successful men give their time, and it includes serving as officers and board members of numerous voluntary organizations. Contributions of money are not enough; the philanthropist is not accorded a leadership role, however vital the money he gives to build schools and libraries and hospitals, if he does not also give his time and thought to community projects. The man who gives only money will be spoken of as a benefactor; he will be praised lavishly on special occasions, as when a building he has donated is opened; but he is not a leader.

This is equally true in the case of foundations, local or national. If the staff of a foundation merely makes grants in accordance with some predetermined plan instead of seeking out unexplored areas of research or need, it is not said to be exercising leadership. And simple, year-in, year-out service in public or private life is also not recognized as leadership. Although people know that it is necessary to have presidents and secretaries and treasurers, teachers who teach and school principals who keep schools going, physicians who tend their patients in good weather and bad, faithful clerks who register wills and births and deaths, none of these maintenance functions are thought of as leadership functions. Leadership is quite literally the function of moving ahead of other people—of seeing something others have not seen and persuading others of its importance.

But if the recognition of its importance comes belatedly, and twenty years later people say, "John was right: he saw what was happening to this town; he talked for years about how that dam was dangerous; he warned us that the West End was turning into slums; he said the plans for the new university stadium were too small; he knew we needed an airport," such a man is not a leader. His endless prophesying and worrying may, indeed, create the climate of opinion within which someone may later get the necessary action under way. But he is not a leader, whether he is a Cassandra preaching doom or an optimist urging the people toward a promised land that he sees clearly but they have not yet glimpsed.

To lead, in American terms, one must be able to mobilize action. There must be co-workers, and the emphasis must be on the program to be carried out, not on the man or woman out in front. The press, always tuned to personalities, plays up personalities and the grip they have on the imagination of their followers, as happens with small sectarian religious movements, daring political movements, and bizarrely radical experiments. It is within such fringe movements that fail, not in new movements that become part of the American scene, that the names of individuals tend to be enshrined. Thus for many Americans Jane Addams' name is associated with the women's peace movement, which she started in an attempt to halt World War I, rather than with the famous settlement house she founded in Chicago (Hull House) or for the myriad tasks she performed on behalf of children, particularly the disadvantaged children of the urban poor, in helping to secure the passage of the first federal child labor law in 1916. Similarly, those who still speak most reverently of Woodrow Wilson are those who shared his terrible feeling of frustration when the United States failed to enter the League of Nations and still think of him as the leader of a great lost cause.

On the political left, people remember the names of Sacco and Vanzetti, minor actors martyred in the atmosphere of political oppression which followed World War

I; on the right, they remember Senator Joseph R. McCarthy as one who tried to protect America from what he believed to be the insidious effects of widespread subversion. The name of Senator J. William Fulbright, who inaugurated the generous idea of using lend-lease credits —money due to the United States for loans made to other countries during World War II—for the international exchange of scholars and students, has passed into our language as a noun. Thousands of students dream of getting "Fulbrights"; hundreds travel on "Fulbrights"; and a "Fulbright" does not mean the senator or one of his family: it means the kind of scholarship he invented. And only a short time after President Kennedy's death, when a whole nation was saddened by bereavement, people began to speak of the "Kennedy Program" as something good in its own right that needed implementing.

If Jane Addams became a figure consulted and respected by a vast network of influential men and women, if Eleanor Roosevelt was a name and a personality to conjure with, it was because of their deep involvement in activities and their effect on what other people did. Thousands of people wrote to Mrs. Roosevelt of their hopes and plans, and she answered them, seriously, respectful of their thoughts and feelings. Much of what her correspondents wanted to do had perhaps been done many times before, in many other places, but their ideas were new to them, and they wanted her voice to say that they were good. Always she responded generously, with sympathy and enthusiasm for their efforts.

Essentially, leaders are people who initiate action, first by proposing that something new be done, then by seeing that it gets done. This is the essence of leadership anywhere: in a small group of adolescents, on the faculty of a university, in the management of an industry, in a farm organization, or in a labor union. Leaders may propose ideas that have been put into action in many other places; their ideas may have been advocated vociferously or plaintively for as much as a generation; but the point is, when leaders assume leadership, something happens and action occurs. To get something done in this way means that the person who is leading must respect those from whom he asks action. The prophet prophesies doom to an erring and wicked people; the preacher admonishes; the demagogue appeals to fear and distrust and hate, or to a sense of exclusiveness (you are superior to others; you are the ones to be saved; others have stolen, are stealing, will steal your birthright). But the American who succeeds in moving a community to action must respect those to whom he or she appeals, because it is only by the call of strength to strength that accomplishments occur among a people who do not respect authority as such, but who respect a person, a cause, a position they believe to be right.

However, because leaders are thought of primarily as persons who can inspire others to take the next step, it does not follow that everyone with leadership responsibility spends all his time on innovations. The democratic leader with too many ideas may lose his hold on his following if he tends to chase wildly after new ideas before the chairman has had time to appoint a committee to consider his last one. Because the orderly processes of democratic action are slow, committees must be appointed, programs must be drawn up, hearings must be conducted, charters must be obtained. No action will succeed that is pushed through too rapidly or with too much agreement.

When a meeting is called to consider a new idea, such as the erection of a new courthouse or the formation of a new organization, if no objections are raised, everyone knows that the meeting was a mere formality, just a gesture to rubber-stamp some program or proposal that someone worked out in advance. A certain kind of unanimity makes people suspicious, ill at ease, and a disgruntled faction is almost certain to form when something important slips through a meeting too easily. Things have to be thrashed out until all the objections are known and everyone has had a chance to speak his mind. Ideas handled in meetings have to be fairly simple, and it is up to someone with leadership ability to make them clear.

Another essential for the person who would lead is the willingness to work harder and for longer hours than those whose support is also needed. This is especially true if leadership is supplied by someone who receives a salary, such as the professional executive of an organization or foundation, or a member of a local government. This kind of leader has to work even harder than he otherwise would be expected to do in order to demonstrate that the thing he believes in is worth working for. A man like Dr. Howard Rusk, who since World War II has been almost solely responsible for the great development of physical medicine—the rehabilitation of many types of handicapped individuals—not only spends his time in national and international councils, but must continue to attend smaller meetings, attend to individual cases, stop and confer with the editors of newspapers, and demonstrate over and over again his continuing human concern for each detail of the vast movement that he has inaugurated. He is a working leader, and in America the work of a working leader is never done.

Because a capacity for hard, continuous, organizational work is part of the equipment of our leaders, many are recruited from those who have had experience in the maintenance activities that keep organizations going. They are persons who realize the work that has to be done routinely and continuously to keep any association alive and moving. A community that is short of leadership usually has few organizations within which young people and older people receive training in such details of organization work as running a meeting, sensing when not to press a point, clarifying an argument, deciding when it is time to make a new proposal. Yet, it is to trained persons in organizations that a community turns, as Galveston did, when it must mobilize for an emergency—a fire or a flood, a war or a depression.

Faced by miles and miles of little "cracker box"

houses, where no person, man or woman, has ever worked responsibly to get something done in harmony with other like-minded or similarly situated individuals, people are likely to say, "There is no leadership here." And they are likely to be wrong, as they were during World War II when leadership sprang from some very unpromising neighborhoods as situations were created that called it forth, such as block organization plans which were dependent for their success on finding the right block leaders.

Furthermore, the leader must be someone who believes that his organization can survive without him. At the first building stage, especially when a community lacks purpose and experience with organization, when a group has been voiceless for a long time, when a new goal must be seen as a vision to be pursued, then a particularly gifted leader is needed. Later, after the battles are fought, the organization well launched, the cause clearly defined, and preferably after the original leader is dead, then some of the vision and excitement and sense of direction that he gave may be recaptured in portraits and statues, in the names of community centers, schools, museums, bridges, and airports. This orderly process of preserving for future generations a sense of the great men and women who have gone before was intensified in the case of President Kennedy, when a people who felt they had been deprived by his death of a vividly experienced leadership with many years to run set about renaming old buildings and erecting new ones that could be named for him, in a flurry of effort to recapture something of what they had lost.

A second kind of balance between the power and influence of the gifted leader and the American preference for distributing power and leadership is found as people move away from, or through, some local community or organization, going up a ladder from local chapter to state, to national levels, and then out altogether onto some other stage. Very few organizations keep their past presidents busy after they leave office. Usually, former presidents, at almost any organizational level, cease being active when they have served their terms.

The idea of a term, a limited but definite commitment on the part of the officers and the membership, whether in a tiny society or in the nation itself, is essential to the American ideal. Leadership is felt to be necessary and crucial, but ideally no man should be irreplaceable, and there should be many candidates—good, competent, possible candidates—for positions. When there are not, when a political party has only one choice, when there is no question at all about who will be chairman of the board or the next state president of an organization or the next governor or the next mayor (not because the present holder of the office is holding it magnificently, but because there are no other suitable candidates to choose among), then that community, that organization, that state, the nation itself is in trouble.

In the creation of the United States as a new nation, the founders saved themselves from the guilt of rebellion against their king in two ways: by declaring that the colonies were a separate nation, grown to adulthood, ready for self-government, and by putting a President with a limited term as head of state. Fidelity to the idea of only two fixed terms for the President of the United States (abandoned only once, in wartime, in the case of Franklin D. Roosevelt), and now fixed by law as well as custom, sets the intrinsic leadership style for America: a choice among candidates, a term in which the successful candidate is given scope and faithful cooperation, an end to his holding that particular position. All these embody the firm belief that ultimate power lies in the people, and that no single man or woman is indispensable.

When a city languishes under terrible mismanagement for many years, and everyone recalls the mayor who once made it work, this is not an indictment of a situation that produces few men who would make good mayors, but a revelation of the deplorable state of the city which is incapable, as an organization, of attracting anyone worthy of the honor of being its chief administrative officer. In the United States, more often perhaps than in many other countries, just because the field is so open, people get the leaders they deserve. It is the people who provide the opportunity. It is the people who make the hour. The man who becomes the leader is a man who *meets* the hour, but he does not make it.

Living under the American system means living always with a series of compromises that make freedom really possible, freedom to fail as well as freedom to succeed. Progress comes through the slow establishment of new standards of justice, of welfare, of education, of opportunity, below which we are no longer willing to let any group fall. These new standards place a floor under all American activities. Great historic documents, such as England's Magna Carta and the American Declaration of Independence, place a floor under the whole concept of political rights and privileges, a level below which no individual should be expected to fall. Our more modern national legislation is placing a floor below which no individual should fall in terms of well-being and opportunity. It is important to note, however, that although this legislation sets the lower limits—minimum standards of living for the nation as a whole—it sets no ceilings. Every community is free to hitch its wagon to the brightest star in sight, to be as good as local initiative can make it.

Only when a program for the betterment of the health or welfare of the country is actually met by leadership within the groups to be benefited can it possibly succeed. Slaves were freed, Indians were given land to live on, slum dwellers were provided with new housing. But not until they themselves took their fate into their own hands did they begin to build a good life for themselves. However much the original leadership for a good cause may be a response to an aroused public conscience to which some imaginative national leader has given shape, activities conducted on behalf of nonparticipating people fail in the long run. Take the social worker or the welfare worker who comes from outside and ascertains people's needs and brings in relief and counseling: If that social worker cannot establish local organization and local leadership, he eventually arouses resentment and distrust. Eternally alert to see that our rights are not invaded, Americans characteristically call all of their voluntary organizations *private* and consider them part of their own private lives—the part that is more theirs than any public and more distant form of organization.

So the recurrent task of leadership in America is to help groups that have been voiceless—the young, the aged, the poor, the isolated, the dreamers of dreams— to find, each in its own way, voices and forms of organization that will yield the excitement of self-realization. Those leaders are especially remembered who have recognized this need for self-expression, and have included stirring pleas for effort and initiative in the words with which they have aroused other people to action. In the United States, unless government and voluntary activities are not only *of* the people and *for* the people but also *by* the people, the people suffer. The business of democracy is never finished. Each obstacle surmounted in the struggle for human dignity and freedom leads to recognition of other obstacles to be overcome on the way to the goal. But as long as the star toward which the wagon is moving is clearly visible, the obstacles, in themselves, are unimportant. It is peoples without vision who perish.

INDEX

draft and voting, 141-3
dress, restrictions by, 156-7

E

Eastern Orthodox Church, 146
Economic Opportunities Act of 1964, 46-7, 97-8
education, compulsory, 115
education, experimental, 172-3
Eisenhower, Milton S., 74
Ellis Island, 42

F

Farmer-Stockman, 77-79
Federal Office of Economic Opportunity, 98
Federal Office of Manpower, Automation, and Training, 98
Ford Foundation, 74
foundations, 133-8
fraternities and sororities, 160-61
Fredericktown (Winchester), Virginia, 27
Fulbright, Senator J. William, 209
Fund for Adult Education, 73-4

G

Galveston plan, 14-15
Garcia, Lauro, 96
GO (Guadalupe Organization), 96-8
"Good Hope Corner," 92
grandfather clause, 153
group activities, 23-4
Guadalupe, Arizona, 28, 93
Guadalupe Organization, *see* GO
Gwaltney, J. J., 184
Gypsies, 149-50

H

Haddonfield, New Jersey, 51

Hawaii, 22
Hearst, Phoebe Apperson, 190
Hedrick, Wyatt, 79
Holland, Virginia, 183
Home Demonstration Clubs, 75, 84-5
honorary memberships, 154
Huguenots, 17, 38, 148

I

immigration laws, 106-7
Industrial Areas Foundation of Chicago, 95
Institute for Intercultural Studies, 9
internal migration, 45-7

J

James I, 49
Jamestown Colony, 15, 20, 49
Japanese-Americans, relocation of, 40-41
Jefferson, Thomas, 114
Jesuits, 145
Jewish communities, 148

K

Kiwanis, 24
Knights of Labor, 115

L

leadership, 205, 209
life memberships, 154
Lions Club, 24
Loudoun County Home Demonstration Clubs, 84
Loudoun County, Virginia, 81

M

Magdalen Society, 134

Massachusetts, 20-21
Massachusetts Bay Colony, 20
Mayflower, 16
Mayflower Compact, 25
McKee, Elmore M., 71-4, 99
membership, community, 102, 108
Mennonites, 17, 38, 148
Moravians, 17, 38, 148

N

Nansemond County, Virginia, 183
National Assn. for Retarded Children, 178-83
National Broadcasting Company, 73
National Congress of Parents and Teachers, 187
national organizations v. local, 152-3
national origins, diversity of, 37-40
National Travelers Aid Assn., 192
naturalization, 129
nepotism, 168-9
New Haven, 20-21
New Jersey Provincial legislature, 105
New Plymouth, 20-21
New York Travelers Aid Society, 193
Niebuhr, Reinhold, 144
North Philadelphia, Pennsylvania, 85

O

Office of Education, 179
Opportunities Industrialization Center, Inc., 86, 89, 92, 93
organizations, structure of, 129-33

P

Parent-Teacher Assn., 187

Penn, William, 27
Philadelphia Chamber of Commerce, 88
Philadelphia City Council, 88
Philadelphia Council for Community Advancement, 88-9
physical appearance, differences in, 44-5
Pilgrims, 15-18, 28, 38, 148
Plymouth Colony, 15-17, 20
political refugees, 42-3
population growth, 30-31
Presbyterian Church of the United States, 95
private schools, 121, 123-5, 172
PTA, *see* National Congress of Parents and Teachers
PTA Magazine, 191
Puritans, 17, 28, 148

Q

Quakers, 17, 23, 27, 38, 148
quota system, elimination of, 42

R

rehabilitation, inner city, 34-5
religious orders, 145-8
residence restrictions, 110-12
Reston, Virginia, 62
Ritter, Rev. Thomas J., 87
Robinson, Jackie, 91
Roman Catholic Church, 146
Roosevelt, Eleanor, 209
Roosevelt, Franklin D., 205
Ross, Fred, 95
Rotary International, 24
Rural Electrification Administration, 77
Ruritan National, 24, 183
Rusk, Dr. Howard, 211

S

school systems, 114-26

The Authors

Dr. Margaret Mead and Dr. Muriel Brown are internationally known for the contributions they have made, as cultural anthropologist and psychologist, to programs and conferences in the United States and around the world. Their counsel is most often sought in situations that involve problems of family life and community development.

It was their mutual interest in American wartime community organization that first brought these two social scientists together in 1942, in Washington, D.C., when they were both working with the Committee on Food Habits of the National Research Council, Dr. Mead as Executive Secretary and Dr. Brown as a liaison member representing the United States Office of Education.

Early in the years of World War II, Dr. Mead wrote *And Keep Your Powder Dry,* a study of the ability of Americans to sustain the war effort and forge from it ideas and experiences of lasting value. In 1942 and 1943, Dr. Brown prepared two handbooks for community workers: *Democracy Means All of Us—How Communi-*

ties Organize to Study and Meet Community Needs, and *The Schools and Community Organization*.

In 1949, Dr. Mead prepared a manual for the United Nations Educational, Scientific, and Cultural Organization, *Cultural Patterns and Technical Change*, and since has served as consultant on policies and programs relating to community development, both for the United States government and for a number of international groups, including UNESCO, the World Health Organization, and the World Federation for Mental Health.

Between 1949 and 1957, Dr. Brown undertook several assignments under the auspices of government agencies and private foundations to help with programs of family-life education and community development in Germany, Egypt, and Pakistan. In 1954, the United States Office of Education published her book, *With Focus on Family Living*, the story of four experimental programs in community organization for family-life education carried on in four different parts of the country.

The authors feel that *The Wagon and the Star* is a book neither one would have written alone, for the experiences on which it draws are complementary and different. Here Dr. Mead and Dr. Brown have attempted to distill what they have learned in working closely with communities of many kinds, and with government agencies and leaders in old and new nations faced with critical problems of community organization.

Because they have spent so much time listening to questions brought up at conference tables in different countries, both authors know how difficult it sometimes is for people of other nationalities to understand American community organization, especially when the organizers are volunteers who work with no thought of monetary gain. The American belief that *anyone* can and should volunteer to take the initiative when a community problem needs to be solved is strange doctrine to many a person who has grown up in a culture where tradition has dictated, for centuries, the place of the individual in the community and the part he is expected, or not expected, to play in community life.

Americans are so committed to the idea of individual responsibility for community action that when they visit other countries and are shown villages without schools or hospital facilities, they ask, "Why don't *you* change these conditions? Why don't *you* do something about this?" *The Wagon and the Star* discusses the reasons for this American attitude, explains why Americans take it for granted that anyone can volunteer to try to change—and may, indeed, be able to start a train of events that will change—community situations needing correction. The question "Why don't *you* do something about it?" is the beginning of the voluntary process by which Americans not only get things done, but in the doing, shape and reshape their communities, hoping to come closer with each reshaping to the stars that are their goals.

Printed in U.S.A.